James Riker

Evacuation Day, 1783, its Many Stirring Events

James Riker

Evacuation Day, 1783, its Many Stirring Events

ISBN/EAN: 9783744681063

Printed in Europe, USA, Canada, Australia, Japan

Cover: Foto ©ninafisch / pixelio.de

More available books at **www.hansebooks.com**

EVACUATION DAY,

1783,

ITS

MANY STIRRING EVENTS:

WITH

RECOLLECTIONS

OF

CAPT. JOHN VAN ARSDALE,

OF THE VETERAN CORPS OF ARTILLERY,

BY WHOSE EFFORTS ON THAT DAY

THE ENEMY WERE CIRCUMVENTED,

AND

THE AMERICAN FLAG SUCCESSFULLY RAISED ON THE BATTERY.

WITH ILLUSTRATIVE NOTES.

BY

JAMES RIKER,

Author of the Annals of Newtown, and History of Harlem ; Life Member of the
New York Historical Society, Etc.

PRINTED FOR THE AUTHOR.

NEW YORK

1883.

CRICHTON & CO.,
PRINTERS,
221-225 Fulton St., N. Y.

EVACUATION DAY.

CHAPTER I

OUR MEMORABLE REVOLUTION, so prolific of grand and glorious themes, presents none more thrilling than is afforded by the closing scene in that stupendous struggle which gave birth to our free and noble Republic. New York City will have the honor of celebrating, on the 25th of November, the hundredth anniversary of this event, the most signal in its history; and which will add the last golden link to the chain of Revolutionary Centennials. A century ago, on "Evacuation Day," so called in our local calendar, the wrecks of those proud armies,—sent hither by the mother country to enforce her darling scheme of "taxation without representation,"—withdrew from our war-scarred city, with the honors of *defeat* thick upon them, but leaving our patriotic fathers happy in the enjoyment of their independence, so gloriously won in a seven years' conflict.

With the expiring century has also disappeared the host of brave actors in that eventful drama! Memory, if responsive, may bring up the venerable forms of the "Old Seventy Sixers," as they still lingered among us two score years ago; and perchance recall with what soul-stirring pathos they oft rehearsed "the times that tried men's souls." But they have fallen, fallen before the last great enemy, till not one is left to repeat the story of their campaigns, their sufferings, or their triumphs. But shall their memories perish, or their glorious deeds pass into oblivion? Heaven forbid! Rather let us treasure them in our heart of hearts, and speak their praises to our children; thus may we keep unimpaired our love of country, and kindle the patriotism of those who come after us. To-day they shall live again, in the event we celebrate. And what event can more strongly appeal to the popular gratitude than that which brought our city a happy deliverance from a foreign power, gave welcome relief to our patriot sires, who had fought for their country or suffered exile, and marked the close of a struggle which conferred the priceless blessings of peace and liberty, and a government which knows no sovereign but the people only. Our aim shall be, not so much to impress the reader with the moral grandeur of that day, or with its historic significance as bearing upon the subsequent growth and prosperity of our great metropolis; but the rather to present a popular account of what occurred at or in connection with the evacuation; and also to satisfy a curiosity often expressed to know something more of a former citizen, much esteemed in his time, whose name, from an incident which then took place, is inseparably associated with the scenes of Evacuation Day.

At the period referred to, a century ago, the City of New York contained a population of less than twenty thousand souls, who mostly resided below Wall Street, above which the city was not compactly built; while northward of the City Hall Park, then known as the Fields, the Commons, or the Green, were little more than scattered farm houses and rural seats. The seven years' occupation by the enemy had reduced the town to a most abject condition; many of the church edifices having been desecrated and applied to profane uses; the dwellings, which their owners had vacated on the approach of the enemy, being occupied by the refugee loyalists, and officers and attachés of the British army, were despoiled and delapidated; while a large area of the City, ravaged by fires, still lay in ruins!

The news of peace with Great Britain, which was officially published at New York on April 8th, 1783, was hailed with delight by every friend of his country. But it spread consternation and dismay among the loyalists. Its effects upon the latter class, and the scenes which ensued, beggar all description. The receipt of death warrants could hardly have been more appalling. Some of these who had zealously taken up commissions in the king's service, amid the excitement of the hour tore the lapels from their coats and stamped them under foot, crying out that they were ruined forever! Others, in like despair, uttered doleful complaints, that after sacrificing their all, to prove their loyalty, they should now be left to shift for themselves, with nothing to hope for, either from king or country. In the day of their power these had assumed the most insolent bearing towards their fellow-citizens who were suspected of sympathy for their suffering country; while those thrown among them as prisoners of war, met their studied scorn and abuse, and were usually accosted, with the more popular than elegant epithet, of "damned rebel!" The tables were now turned; all this injustice and cruelty stared them in the face, and, to their excited imaginations, clothed with countless terrors that coming day, when, their protectors being gone, they could expect naught but a dreadful retribution! Under such circumstances, Sir Guy Carleton, the English commander at New York, was in honor bound not to give up the City till he had provided the means of conveying away to places within the British possessions, all those who should decide to quit the country. It was not pure humanity, but shrewd policy as well, for the king, by his agents, thus to promote the settlement of portions of his dominions which were cold, barren, uninviting, and but sparsely populated.

By the cessation of hostilities the barriers to commercial intercourse between the City and other parts of the State, &c., were removed, and the navigation of the Hudson, the Sound, and connected waters was resumed as before the war. Packets brought in the produce of the country, and left laden with commodities suited to the needs of the rural population, or with the British gold in their purses; for all the staples of food, as flour, beef, pork and butter, were in great demand, to victual the many fleets preparing to sail, freighted with troops, or with loyalists. The country people in the vicinity also flocked to the public markets, bringing all kinds of provisions, which they readily sold at moderate rates for hard cash; and thus the adjacent country was supplied and enriched with specie. The fall in prices, which during the war had risen eight hundred per cent, brought a most grateful relief to the consumers. Simultaneously with these tokens of better days, the order for the release of all the prisoners of war from the New York prisons and prisonships, with their actual liberation from their gloomy cells, came as a touching reminder that the horrors of war were at an end.

Many of the old citizens who had fled, on or prior to the invasion of the City by the British, and had purchased homes in the country, now prepared to return, by selling or disposing of these places, expecting upon reaching New York to re-occupy their old dwellings, without let or hindrance, but on arriving here were utterly astonished at being debarred their own houses; the commandant, General Birch, holding the keys of all dwellings vacated by persons leaving, and only suffering the owners to enter their premises as tenants, and upon their paying him down a quarter's rent in advance! Such apparent injustice determined many not to come before the time set for the evacuation of the City, while many others were kept back through fear of the loyalists, whose rage and vindictiveness were justly to be dreaded. Hence, though our people were allowed free ingress and egress to and from the City, upon their obtaining a British pass for that purpose, yet but few, comparatively, ventured to bring their families or remain permanently till they could make their entry with, or under the protection of, the American forces.

Never perhaps in the history of our City had there been a corresponding period of such incessant activity and feverish excitement. Stimulated by their fears, the loyalist families began arrangements in early spring for their departure from the land of their birth (indeed a company of six hundred, including women and children, had already gone the preceding fall) destined mainly for Port Roseway, in Nova Scotia, where they ultimately formed their principal settlement, and built the large town of Shelburne. Those intending to remove were required to enter their name, the number in their family, &c., at the Adjutant-General's Office, that due provision might be made for their passage. They flocked into the City in such numbers from within the British lines (and many from within our lines also) that often during that season there were not houses enough to shelter them. Many occupied huts made by stretching canvass from the ruined walls of the burnt districts. They banded together for removing, and had their respective headquarters, where they met to discuss and arrange their plans. The first considerable company, some five thousand, sailed on April 27th, and larger companies soon followed. Many held back, hoping for some act of grace on the part of our Legislature which would allow them to stay. But the public sentiment being opposed to it, and expressed in terms too strong to be disregarded, these at last had to yield to necessity, and find new homes. The mass of the loyalists went to Nova Scotia and Canada; others to the Island of Abaco, in the Bahamas; while not a few of the more distinguished or wealthy retired to England. The bitterness felt towards this class was to be deplored, but, in truth, the active part taken by many of them during the war against their country, and above all the untold outrages committed upon defenceless inhabitants by tories (the zealous and active loyalists), often in league with Indians, had kindled a resentment towards all loyalists alike that stifled every philanthrophic feeling. This exodus was going on when General Carleton, about the beginning of August, received his final orders for the evacuation of the City; but it took nearly four months more to complete it, as a large number of vessels were required to transport the immense crowds of refugees who left with their families and effects during that brief period. Hundreds of slaves (ours being then a slave State) were also induced to go to *Nory Koshee*, as they called it. Their masters could do little to hinder it, though a committee appointed by both governments to superintend all embarkations did something towards preventing slaves and other property belonging to our people from being carried away. Such negroes as had been found in a state of freedom, General Carleton held, had a right to leave if they chose to do so, and many probably got away under this pretext; but to provide against mistakes the name of each negro (with that of his former owner) was registered, and also such facts as would fix his value, in case compensation were allowed. In this, as in the whole ordering of the evacuation, which was more than the work of a day, General Carleton must have credit for humanity and a disposition to pursue a fair and honorable course, which, under the extraordinary difficulties of

the situation, required rare tact and discretion. Of course he
was blamed for much when he was not responsible (natural
enough in those who suffered grievances), and especially for the
great delay in giving up the City, which bore hard on virtuous
citizens who had sacrificed opulence and ease at the shrine of
liberty, and had now thrown themselves out of homes and business in the expectation of an early return to the City. Yet
Carleton's fidelity to the various trusts committed to him, making
one delay after another unavoidable, it may be doubted whether
he could have surrendered the City at an earlier date.

Closing up the affairs of the army was truly a Herculean task.
The shipment of the troops began early in the season. A portion
of the army was disbanded to reduce it to a peace establishment
pursuant to orders from England. Then there was the settlement of innumerable accounts, pertaining to every department,
and the sale and disposal of surplus army property, as horses,
wagons, harness and military stores, with several thousand cords
of fire wood, which was sold off at half its cost. Even the
prisonships were set up at auction. A sale of draft horses was
begun, October 2d, at the Artillery Stables near St. Paul's church.

Auctions on private account were rife ; daily, in every street,
the red flag was seen hanging out. And it was alleged that a great
deal of furniture was sold to which the venders had no good title ;
much of it being newly painted or otherwise disguised, that its
proper owner might never know and reclaim it ! We need not
doubt it, for it seemed as if the refugees would strip the City of
every portable article, even to the buildings, or the brick and
lumber composing them ; insomuch that the authorities, in formal
orders, forbade the removal or demolition of any house till the
right to do so was shown.

These irregularities, with the brag and bluster of the enraged
tories, was enough to keep society in a broil. The uppermost
themes were the evacuation, and the removal to Nova Scotia, or
elsewhere. They were irritating topics, and gave rise to endless
and hot discussions, in which tory vexed tory. While one maintained that Nova Scotia was a very Paradise, another denounced
it as unfit for human beings to inhabit. Disappointed and cha-
grined at the issue of the war, they would curse the powers to
whom they owed allegiance ; as rebellious as those they called
rebels. In other cases, the turn the war had taken had a magic
effect upon their principles ; once avowed loyalists, they suddenly
became zealous patriots ! It was a witty reply given by a tailor,—the tailor, in the olden time, we must premise, was often
applied to, to rip up and turn a coat, when threadbare or faded.
" How does business go on ? " asked a friend. " Not very well,"
said he, " my customers have all learned to turn their own coats !"

The shrewd whigs were not to be deceived by these sudden conversions. They drew the line nicely at a meeting held on Nov. 18th, at Cape's Tavern, in Broadway, (site of the Boreel Building), to arrange plans for evacuation day. Before touching their business, they " *Resolved*. That every person, whatever his political character may be, who hath remained in this City during the late contest, be requested to leave the room forthwith."

Society could not be very secure, when, as is stated, scarcely a night passed without a robbery ; scarcely a morning came, but corpses were found upon the streets, the work of the assassin or midnight revel. Indeed at this juncture, there was much underlying apprehension in the minds of good citizens ; **the situation was unprecedented**, men's passions had been **wrought** up to a fearful pitch, and **who** could foresee the **outcome!** Sensible of the danger, and with the approval **of** the commandant, a large number of citizens lately returned **from** exile, organized as a guard and patrolled the streets, on the night preceding evacuation day. The vigilance of these returned patriots, and the protection it afforded, added greatly to the public security at this threatening crisis.

A word as to the aspect of **the City ;** sanitary rules being suspended, the public streets were in a most filthy condition. All the churches, except the Episcopal, the Methodist, and the Lutheran (spared to please the Hessians), had been converted into hospitals, prisons, barracks, riding-schools, or storehouses ; the pews, and in some the galleries, torn out, the window-lights broken, and all **foul and** loathesome. **Fences** enclosing the churches and cemeteries had disappeared, and the very graves and tombs lay hidden by rubbish and filth ! No public moneyed or charitable institutions, no insurance offices existed ; trade was at the lowest ebb, education wholly neglected, the schools and college shut up ! But the long-wished-for event, which **was to** light up this dark picture, and work a happy transformation, **was** at hand.

Finally, the day fixed upon for the evacuation, and for the triumphal entry **of** Washington and the American army, to take possession of the city, was Tuesday, the 25th of November. At an early hour, on that cold, but radiant morning, the whole population seemed to be abroad, making ready for the great gala day, regardless of a keen nor'wester. **During** the forenoon many delegations from the suburban districts began **to arrive, to share in** the public festivities, or to witness the exit of the foreign troops, and **the entrance** of the victorious Americans ; while with the latter was expected a host of patriots, to re-occupy their desolate dwellings, from which they had been **so** long cruelly exiled ; or otherwise, only to gaze upon the charred and blackened ruins of what was once their homes !*

To guard against any disturbance which such an occasion might favor, in the interval between the laying down and the resumption of authority, and as rumors were afloat of an organized plot to plunder the town when the King's forces were withdrawn ; the hour of noon had been set for the Royal troops to move, and by an understanding between the two commanders-in-chief, the Americans were to promptly advance and occupy the positions as the British vacated them ; the latter, when ready to move, to send out an officer to notify our advance guard. There was no longer any antagonism between these, so recently hostile, forces ; the plans for the *evacuation*, on the one part, and the *occupation*, on the other, being carried out in as orderly a manner, and to all appearance, with as friendly a spirit, as when, in time of peace, one guard relieves another at a military post.

Major Gen. Knox, a large, fine looking officer, had been appointed to command the American troops which were first to enter and occupy the city. With his forces, consisting of a corps of dragoons, under Capt. John Stakes, another of artillery, and several battalions of infantry, with a rear guard under Major John Burnet, Knox marched from McGown's Pass, Harlem, early in the morning, halting at the present junction of the Bowery and Third Avenue. Here he waited—meanwhile holding a friendly parley with the English officers, whose forces were also resting a little in advance of him—until about one o'clock in the afternoon. The British then receiving orders to move, took up their march, passed down the Bowery and Chatham street, and wheeling into Pearl, finally turned off to the river, and went on shipboard. The American forces under Gen. Knox, following on, proceeded through Chatham street, into and down Broadway, and took possession. As they advanced, greeted with happy faces and joyful acclamations by crowds of freemen who lined the streets, or fairer

---

* THE GREAT FIRE, of September 20, 1776, beginning at Whitehall slip, swept along the river front and northward, consuming all the buildings between Whitehall street on the west and Broad street on the east, extending up Broadway to a point just below Rector street, and up Broad street as far as Beaver, above which the houses on Broad street escaped : the fire being confined to a line nearly straight from Beaver, near Broad, to the point it reached on Broadway. Crossing Broadway, it also swept everything north of Morris street, including Trinity Church ; from which point passing behind the city (later Cape's) Tavern, it spared the line of buildings, mainly dwellings, facing Broadway, with a few joining them on the cross streets, but otherwise made a clean sweep as far up as Barclay street, where the College grounds stayed its further progress.

The fire of August 3, 1778, which was confined to the blocks between Old slip and Coenties slip, reaching up to Pearl street, was a small affair in comparison.

forms drawn to the windows and balconies by the beat of the American drums and the vociferous cheering, the march down Broadway to Cape's Tavern (on the site now of the Boreel Building), was indeed the triumphal march of conquerors!

Our troops having halted and taken their position opposite and below Cape's Tavern,* Gen. Knox quitted them, and heading a body of mounted citizens, lately returned from exile, and who had met by arrangement at the Bowling Green, each wearing in his hat a sprig of laurel, and on the left breast a Union cockade, made of black and white ribbon, rode up into the Bowery to receive their Excellencies General Washington and Governor George Clinton, who were at the Bull's Head Tavern (site of the Thalia Theatre), they having arrived at Day's Tavern, Harlem, on the 21st inst., the very day on which Carleton had drawn in his forces and abandoned the posts from Kingsbridge to McGown's Pass, inclusive.

At the Bull's Head, where the widow Varien presided as hostess, congratulations passed freely, and a series of hearty demonstrations began, on the part of the overjoyed populace, which continued along the whole line of Washington's march, and closed only with the day. The civic procession having formed began its grand entry in the following order:

General Washington, "straight as a dart and noble as he could be," riding a spirited gray horse, and Governor Clinton, on a splendid bay, with their respective suites also mounted; and having as escort a body of Westchester Light Horse, under the command of Capt. Delavan.

The Lieutenant Governor, Pierre Van Cortlandt, with the members of the Council for the temporary Government of the Southern District of New York; four abreast.

Major Gen. Knox, and the officers of the army; eight abreast. Citizens on horseback; eight abreast.

The Speaker of the Assembly, and citizens on foot; eight abreast.

---

* The orders of Nov. 24, to our troops read: "The Light Infantry will furnish a company for Main Guard to-morrow. As soon as the troops are formed in the city, the Main Guard wil be marched off to Fort George; on their taking possession, an officer of artillery will immediately hoist the American standard. * * * On the standard being hoisted in Fort George, the artillery will fire thirteen rounds. Afterwards his Excellency Governor Clinton will be received on the right of the line. The officers will salute his Excellency as he passes them, and the troops present their arms by corps, and the drums beat a march. After his Excellency is past the line, and alighted at Cape's Tavern, the artillery will fire thirteen rounds."

As our flag was not raised on Fort George, nor the salute fired until after Gov. Clinton and Gen. Washington arrived there, the delay, and failure to carry out the orders strictly as issued, must be accounted for by the embarrassing incident hereafter noticed.

MAP

Showing Washington's line of march from Bull's Head (Bowery), to Cape's Tavern, in Broadway; and thence to Fort George.

Near the Tea-water Pump, (in Chatham street **just** above **Pearl),** where the citizens on foot had gathered to join **the pro-cession,** Washington halted the column, while Gen. Knox and **the** officers of the Revolution drew **out** and, forming into line, marched down Chatham **street,** passing a **body of the** British troops which were still halting in the **fields** (now the City Hall Park) ; while Washington and the rest, turning down Pearl street, proceeded on to Wall **street,** and up **Wall,** then **the seat of** fashionable residences, **to** Broadway, **where** both **companies** again met, **and** while **our** troops in line fired a *feu-de-joie,* alighted at the popular tavern before mentioned, **kept by John Cape, where** now stands the Boreel Building.*

We must mention here, **that** when Gen. Knox reached **the New Jail,** then known as the Provost (and now **the Hall of Records), Capt.** Cunningham, the Provost Marshall, **and his** deputy **and jailor** Sergeant Keefe, both having held **those** positions during most of the war, and equally notorious for their brutal treatment **of** the American prisoners who were confined there, thought it about **time** to retreat ; and quitting the jail, followed by the hangman **in his** yellow jacket, passed between a platoon **of** British soldiers **and marched** down Broadway, with the last detachment **of their troops. When** Sergeant Keefe was in the act of **leaving the Provost,** (says John Pintard), one of the few **prisoners then in his custody** for criminal offences, called out : "**Sergeant, what is to become** of us ?" "**You** may all go to the **devil together,"** was his surly reply, **as he** threw **the** bunch of keys **on the floor behind** him. "Thank you, Sergeant," was the cutting **retort,** "**we** have had too much of your company in *this* world, **to wish to** follow you **to the** *next !* " Another incident, which respected Cunningham, **was** witnessed (says **Dr.** Lossing), by the late **Dr. Alexander Anderson.** It was

---

* Why "**the officers of** the Revolution" should **have** taken a different **rout admits** of this explanation. The officers referred to were no doubt **the mounted citizens who** had ridden up **with** Knox from Bowling Green, **among whom** were colonels, captains, etc., of the late army. The move was evidently made to reach Cape's Tavern first, and be in position ready to **receive** their Excellencies, Washington and Clinton, and present addresses, **which** had been prepared. This is referred to in a **letter** written by Elisha D. Whitlesey, dated Danbury, Conn., **Aug. 24, 1821,** "A committee had been appointed by the citizens to wait upon Gen. Washington and **Gov.** Clinton and other American officers, and to express their joyful congratulations to them upon the occasion. A procession for this purpose formed in the Bowery, marched through a part of the city, and halted at **a** tavern, then known by the name of Cooper's [Cape's] **Tavern, in** Broadway, where the following addresses were delivered.* ,**Mr. Thomas** Tucker, late of this town [Danbury], and at that time a respectable merchant in New York, a member of the committee, **was** selected to perform the office on the **part** of the committee."

* **For that** to Washington, and his reply, see next note.

during the forenoon, that a tavern keeper in Murray street hung
out the Stars and Stripes. **Informed of it**, thither hastened
Cunningham, who with **an oath**, and in his imperious tone, ex-
claimed, "Take in that flag, **the** City is **ours** till noon." **Suit-**
ing the action **to the** word, he tried to pull down **the** obnoxious
ensign ; **but** the landlady coming to the rescue, **with** broom
in hand, dealt the Captain such lusty blows, as made the
powder fly in clouds from his **wig**, and forced him to beat a retreat ! The Provost Guard, **and the Main** Guard at the City
Hall (Wall street, opposite Broad, where the U. S. Treasury
stands), were the last to abandon their posts, and repair on shipboard.

The brief reception being over, at Cape's Tavern, (with **pre-**
senting of addresses to Gen. Washington **and Gov.** Clinton), the
cavalcade again formed, and marched to the Battery, to enact
the last formality in re-possessing the City, which was to unfurl
the American flag over Fort George* A great concourse of people **had** assembled, **not** only to witness this ceremony, but to
obtain a sight of the illustrious Washington and other **great**
generals, who had so nobly defended our liberties.

But now a sight was presented, which, **as soon** as **fully under-**
stood, drew forth from the astonished **and** incensed beholders
execrations loud and deep. **The royal ensign was** still **floating**

---

* **ADDRESS** TO **GENERAL WASHINGTON,**
Presented at Cape's Tavern.

To his Excellency GEORGE WASHINGTON, Esquire, General and Commander in Chief of the Armies of the United States of America :

The Address **of** the Citizens of New York, who have returned
from exile, in behalf of themselves and their suffering
brethren :

SIR :

At a moment when the arm of tyranny is yielding **up its fondest**
usurpations, we hope the salutations of long suffering **exiles, but now**
happy freemen, will not be deemed **an** unworthy tribute. **In this**
place, and at this moment of exultation and triumph, while the ensigns
of slavery still linger in our sight, **we** look up to you, our deliverer,
with unusual transports of gratitude **and** joy. Permit **us** to welcome
you to this City, long torn from **us by** the hard hand of oppression,
but **now** by your wisdom and energy, under the guidance of Provi-
dence, once more the seat **of** peace and freedom. We forbear to speak
our gratitude or your praise, we should but **echo** the voice of applaud-
ing millions; but the Citizens of **New** York are eminently indebted **to**
your virtues, and we **who** have now the honor to address your Excellency, have been often companions of your sufferings, and witnesses of
your exertions. Permit us therefore to approach your Excellency with
the dignity and sincerity of freemen, and to assure you that we shall
preserve with **our** latest breath our gratitude **for** your services, and
veneration for your character. And accept of our sincere and earnest
wishes **that** you may long enjoy that calm domestic felicity which you
have so generously sacrificed; that the cries of injured liberty may

as usual over Fort George ; the enemy having departed without striking their colors, though they had dismantled the fort and removed on shipboard all their stores and heavy ordnance, while other cannon lay dismounted under the walls as if thrown off in a spirit of wantonness. On a closer view it was found that the flag had been nailed to the staff, the halyards taken away, and the pole itself besmeared with grease; obviously to prevent or hinder the removal of the emblem of royalty, and the raising of the Stars and Stripes. Whether to escape the mortification of seeing our flag supplant the British standard, or to annoy and exasperate our people were the stronger impulse, it were hard to say. It was too serious for a joke, however, and the dilemma caused no little confusion. The artillery had taken a position on the Battery, the guns were unlimbered, and the gunners stood ready to salute our

---

nevermore interrupt your repose, and that your happiness may be equal to your virtues.

Signed at the request of the meeting.

THOMAS RANDALL.
DAN. PHŒNIX.
SAML. BROOME.
THOS. TUCKER.
HENRY KIPP.
PAT. DENNIS.
WM. GILBERT, **Sr.**
WM. GILBERT, Jr.
FRANCIS VAN DYCK.
JEREMIAH WOOL.
GEO. JANEWAY.
ABRA'm P. LOTT.
EPHRAIM BRASHIER.

NEW YORK, Nov. 25th, 1783.

THE GENERAL'S REPLY.

To the Citizens of New York who have returned from exile :

GETNLEMEN—

I thank you sincerely for your affectionate address, and entreat you to be persuaded that nothing could be more agreeable to me than your polite congratulations. Permit me in turn to felicitate you on the happy repossession of your City.

Great as your joy must be on this pleasing occasion, it can scarcely exceed that which I feel at seeing you, Gentlemen, who from the noblest motives have suffered a voluntary exile of many years, return again in peace and triumph, to enjoy the fruits of your virtuous conduct.

The fortitude and perseverance, which you and your suffering brethren have exhibited in the course of the war, have not only endeared you to your countrymen, but will be remembered with admiration and applause to the latest posterity.

May the tranquility of your City be perpetual,—may the ruins soon be repaired, commerce flourish, science be fostered, and all the civil and social virtues be cherished in the same illustrious manner which formerly reflected so much credit on the inhabitants of New York. In fine, may every species of felicity attend you, Gentlemen, and your worthy fellow citizens.

GEO. WASHINGTON.

colors. But the grease baffled all attempts to shin up the staff. To cut the staff down and erect another would consume too much time. Impatient of delay, "three or four guns were fired with the colors on a pole before they were raised .on the flag-staff."* But this expedient was premature and humiliating, while the hostile flag yet waved as if in defiance. The scene grew exciting : and now appeared another actor, hitherto looking on, but no idle observer of what was passing. He was a young man of medium height, whose ruddy honest face, tarpaulin cap and pea-jacket told his vocation. Born neither to fortune nor to fame, yet by his own merits and exertions he had won the regard of some in that assembly, having served under McClaughry, and Willett, and Weissenfels, as also the Clintons, to whom he had lived neighbor, within that patriotic circle in old Orange, where these were the guiding spirits, and every yeoman with them, shoulder to shoulder, in the common cause. As a subaltern officer he had made a good record during the war, and none present, however superior in station, had sustained a better character or exhibited a purer patriotism. This was John Van Arsdale, late a Sergeant in Capt. Hardenburgh's company of New York Levies. At nineteen years of age, quitting his father's vessel, where he had been bred a sailor, he enlisted in the Continental Army at the beginning of the war, and had served faithfully till its close. Suffering cold and hardship in the Canada expedition, wounded and taken prisoner at the battle of Fort Montgomery, he had languished weary months in New York dungeons, and in the foul hold of a British prisonship, and subsequently braved the perils of Indian warfare in several campaigns. And with such a record, where expect to find him but among his old compatriots, on this day of momentous import, when the struggles of seven years were to culminate in a final triumph.

Van Arsdale volunteered to climb the staff, though with little prospect of succeeding better than others, especially when after making an attempt, sailor fashion, he was unable to maintain his grasp upon the slippery pole. Now it was proposed to replace the cleats which had been knocked off ; and persons ran in haste to Peter Goelet's hardware store, in Hanover Square, and returned with a saw, hatchet, gimlets, and nails. Then willing hands sawed pieces of board, split and bored cleats, and began to nail them on. By this means Van Arsdale got up a short distance, with a line to which our flag was attached ; but just then, a ladder being brought to his assistance, he mounted still higher, then completed the ascent in the usual way, and reaching the top of the staff, tore down the British standard, and rove the new halyards by which the

---

* Gen. Jeremiah Johnson, who was present, so stated to the writer, Feb. 15, 1848.

Star-spangled Banner was quickly run up by Lieut. Anthony
Glean, and floated proudly, while the multitude gave vent to their
joy in hearty cheers, and the artillery boomed forth a national
salute of thirteen guns!*   On descending, Van Arsdale was

---

* A patriotic song was composed for that day, entitled, "The Sheep
Stealers," which was distributed and sung with immense gusto in the
evening coteries.   Coarse, but designed to cast ridicule on the enemy,
it is given as a specimen of the popular songs of the period :

> KING GEORGE sent his Sheep-stealers,
>   Poor Refugees and Tories !
> King George sent his Sheep-stealers
>   To fish for mutton here,
>   To fish for mutton here,
>   To fish for mutton here,
> But Yankees were hard dealers,
>   Poor Refugees and Tories ;
> But Yankees were hard dealers,
>   They sold their sheep-skins dear,
>   They sold their sheep-skins dear,
>   They sold their sheep-skins dear,
> But Yankees were hard dealers,
>   They sold their sheep-skins dear!
>
> At Boston Britons glorious,
>   The Refugees and Tories,
>   Made war on pigs and fowls,
> But o'er men un-victorious,
>   They fled by night like owls !
>
> The Howes came in a huff, Boys,
>   With Refugees and Tories,
>   To plunder, burn and sink ;
> But like a candle-snuff, Boys,
>   They went—and left a stink !
>
> Burgoyne, that cunning rogue, ah !
>   With Refugees and Tories,
>   Of conquest laid grand schemes ;
> But Gates at Saratoga,
>   Awak'd him from his dreams !
>
> The noble Earl Cornwally,
>   With Refugees and Tories,
>   Of southern plunderers chief,
> At Yorktown wept the folly
>   Of stealing "Rebel" beef !
>
> Clinton, that son of thunder,
>   With Refugees and Tories,
>   At New York took his stand,
> And swore that he asunder
>   Would shake the Rebel land !
>
> Of mighty deeds achieving,
>   With Refugees and Tories,
>   He talked, O ! *he* talked big,
> But changed his plan to thieving
>   Of turkey, goose and pig !

warmly greeted by the overjoyed spectators, for the service he
had rendered; but some one proposing a more substantial ac-
knowledgement than mere applause, hats were passed around,
and a considerable sum collected, nearly all within reach contrib-
uting, even to the Commander-in-Chief. Though taken quite
aback, **Van Arsdale** modestly accepted the gift, with a protest at
being rewarded for so trivial an act. But the contributors weer
of another opinion; he had accomplished what was thought impracticable, and the occasion and the emergency made his success
peculiarly gratifying to all present. On returning home to his
amiable Polly (they had been married short of six months), the
story of "Evacuation Day," and the silver money which he
poured into her lap, caused her to open her eyes, and fixed the
circumstance indellibly in her memory!

But to return: during the scene on the Battery, which con-
sumed full an hour, the last squads of the British were getting
into their boats, while many others, filled with soldiers, rested
on their oars between the shore and their ships, anchored in the
North River. They kept silence during this time, and watched
our efforts to hoist the colors (no doubt enjoying our embarrass-
ment), but when our flag was run up and the salute fired, they
rowed off to their shipping, which soon weighed anchor and proceeded down the bay.*

This scene over, the Commander-in-Chief and the general officers, accompanied Gov. Clinton to Fraunces' Tavern, also a
popular resort, and which still stands on the corner of Pearl and
Broad streets. Here the Governor gave a sumptuous dinner.
The repast over, then came "the feast of reason and the flow of
soul," when the sentiments dearest to those brave and loyal men
found utterance in the following admirable toasts:

1. The United States of America.

Of conquest then despairing,
 With Refugees and Tories,
 George for his Bull-dogs sent;
They Yankee vengeance fearing,
 Greased the flag-staff—and went!

Then Yorkers, let's remember
 The Refugees and Tories,
 The five and twentieth day
Of the bleak month, November,
 When the Cow-thieves sneaked away!

* The British troops did not take their final departure from Long
Island and Staten Island till the 4th of December. Their flag waved
over Governor's Island till the 3d, when the Island was formally given
up to an officer sent over by Gov. Clinton, for that purpose. (Mag. of
Am. Hist., 1883, p. 430.) Sir Guy Carleton and other officers and
gentlemen sailed in the frigate Ceres, Capt. Hawkins.

2. His most Christian Majesty.

3. The United Netherlands.

4. The King of Sweden.

5. The American Army.

6. The Fleet and **Armies** of France, which have served in America.

7. The Memory **of those Heroes who have fallen for our Free-dom.**

8. May our Country be grateful to her Military **Children.**

9. May Justice support what Courage has gained.

10. The Vindicators of the Rights of Mankind in every Quarter of the Globe.

11. May America be an Asylum to the Persecuted of the Earth.

12. May a close Union of the States guard the Temple they have erected to Liberty.

13. May the Remembrance of THIS DAY, be a Lesson to Princes.

An extensive illumination of the buildings in the evening, a grand display of rockets, and the blaze of bonfires at every corner, made a fitting sequel to the events of the day.* Great as was the joy, and lively as were the demonstrations of it, not the slightest outbreak or disturbance occurred, to mar the public tranquility ; and the happy citizens retired to rest in the sweet consciousness that the reign of martial law and of regal despotism had ended ! But it was remarked, says an eyewitness of the time, that an unusual proportion of those who in '76 had fled from New York, had been cut off by death and denied a share in the general joy, which marked the return of their fellow citizens to their former habitations. And those habitations, such as had survived the fires, how marred and damaged, as before intimated ; in many cases mere shells and wrecks. And the sanctuaries, where they and their fathers had worshipped, all despoiled, save St. Paul's, St. George's in Beekman street, the Dutch Church, Garden street, the Lutheran church, Frankfort street, the Methodist Meeting House in John street, (none remaining at present but the first and last), and some three or four small and obscure places. Years elapsed, before, in their poverty, the people were enabled fully to restore some of them to their former sacred uses. The churches which suffered most at the enemy's hands were the Middle and North Dutch churches, in Nassau and William streets, the two Presbyterian churches, in Wall and Beekman streets, the Scotch Presbyterian church,

---

* Among the more authentic newspaper accounts of the Evacuation, is one of which I have here availed myself, contained in the New York *Sun* of Nov. 27th, 1859, but copied from the *Observer*. Much valuable material is also **brought** together in the *N. Y. Corp. Manual* for 1870.

in Cedar street, the **French church in Pine street**, the Baptist church, Gold street, **and the Friends' new Meeting** House, in Pearl street; all **since removed** to meet **the demands** of trade. **Religious** affairs **were found in a sad** plight when the evacuation **took place.** The **Dutch, Presbyterian** and Baptist ministers **had gone into voluntary exile.** The Rev. **Charles Inglis**, D.D., **Rector of Trinity Parish, having** made himself very **obnoxious to the patriots, concluded to follow** the loyalists of his flock to **Nova Scotia, and therefore** resigned **his** rectorship Nov. 1st, preceding **the evacuation.** Dr. John H. Livingston, arriving with **our people,** immediately resumed his services in Garden street. **Other** pastors were not so **favored.** Dr. John Rogers, of the **Presbyterian** church, returned **on the** day after the evacuation, and **on the** following Sabbath, Nov. 30th, preached **in St.** George's chapel, " to a thronged and deeply affected assembly," **a** discourse adapted **to the occasion from** Psalms cxvi, 12,—" **What shall** I render unto the Lord, **for all His benefits towards me?"** The vestry of Trinity church having **kindly offered the use of their two** chapels, St. Paul's and St. George's, **the Presbyterians occupied** these buildings **a part** of **every Sabbath until June 27th, 1784,** when **they took possession of the Brick Church, Beekman street, which** had **been** repaired.

On the Friday **following** the evacuation, **the citizens lately** returned from exile, gave an elegant entertainment, **at Cape's** Tavern, to his Excellency, the Governor, and the Council **for governing the City;** when **Gen.** Washington and the Officers of **the** Army, about three **hundred** gentlemen, graced the feast. **The** following Tuesday, **Dec.** 2d, another such entertainment **was** given by Gov. Clinton, **at the same place, to** the French Ambassador, Luzerne, **and in** the evening, at the Bowling Green, the Definitive Treaty **of Peace was** celebrated **by "an** unparalleled exhibition of fireworks," and **when,** says an account of **it,** "the prodigious concourse of spectators **assembled on** the occasion, expressed their plaudits in **loud** and grateful clangors!" On Thursday, the 4th, Gen. **Washington bade a final** adieu to his **fellow** officers at Fraunces' Tavern. **The scene** was most affecting. "With a heart full of love and gratitude," **said** he, "I now **take** leave of you, and most devoutly wish that **your** latter **days may be as** prosperous and happy as your former ones have been glorious and honorable." Embracing each **one in turn, while** tears coursed **down their manly cheeks,** he parted **from them, and from** the City, to **resign his commission to** Congress, and seek again the retirement **of** private life.

The following Thursday, Dec. 11th, was observed by appointment of Congress, "as a day of public Thanksgiving throughout **the** United States." **On** this occasion **Dr.** Rogers preached in

St. George's chapel, a sermon from Psalms cxxvi, 3,—"The Lord hath done great things for us, whereof we are glad." It was afterwards published with the title—"The Divine Goodness displayed in the American Revolution."

Thus just eight score years after Europeans first settled on this Island of Manhattan, our City had its new birth into freedom, and started on its unexampled career of prosperity and greatness. And as we contemplate the growth, enterprise, trade, commerce, credit, opulence and magnificence of the present City, with its hundreds of churches, schools and other noble institutions, and contrast it with the contracted, war-worn, desolate town, of which our fathers took possession on the 25th of November 1783, well may we exclaim—"What hath God wrought?" That day, whose memories were so fondly cherished by our grandsires while they lived, was one of great significance in the history of our City and Country. Its anniversary has ever since been duly celebrated by military parades, and a national salute fired on the Battery at sunrise, by the "Independent Veteran Corps of Heavy Artillery," composed at first of Revolutionary soldiers, and of which John Van Arsdale was long an efficient and honored member, and, at the time of his decease, its First Captain-Lieutenant.* For many

* It caused great surprise, in 1831, that an officer of the Revolution, Capt. John Van Dyck, of Lamb's artillery, who was present at the evacuation of New York, and "was on Fort George and within two feet of the flagstaff," should have stated in the most positive terms, that "there was no British flag on the staff to pull down;" also that no ladder was used, and besides, more than intimated that Van Arsdale did not perform the part ascribed to him! (His letter, in *N. Y. Commercial Advertiser*, of June 30th, 1831.) We well remember Capt. Van Dyck, and do not doubt the sincerity of his statements; but it only shows how effectually facts once well known may be obliterated from the memory by the lapse of time. For few facts in our history are better authenticated than that the royal standard was left flying at the evacuation; and it was afterwards complained of, as the able historian, Mr. Dawson writes me, by John Adams, our first embassador to England, as an unfriendly act, to evacuate the City without a formal surrender of it, or striking their colors. The fact is also mentioned in a pamphlet printed in 1808, by the "Wallabout Committee," (appointed to superintend the interment of the bones of American patriots who perished in the prison ships), and consisting of gentlemen who could not have all been ignorant on such a point, viz., Messrs. Jacob Vandervoort, John Jackson, Issachar Cozzens, Burdet Stryker, Robert Townsend, Jr., Benjamin Watson and Samuel Cowdrey. Hardie, who wrote his account prior to 1825, ("Description of New York," p. 107,) also makes the same statement, and so does Dr. Lossing: "Field Book of the Revolution," 2:633. A letter written in New York *the day after the evacuation*, says "they cut away the halyards from the flagstaff in the fort, and likewise greased the post; so that we *were obliged to have a ladder* to fix a new rope." The use of a ladder is attested by Lieut. Glean; and also by the late Pearson Halstead, who witnessed the ascent. Mr. Halstead stated this to me, in 1845, and that, about the year 1805, he was informed that Van Arsdale was the person who climbed the staff. His association with Mr. Van Arsdale, both in busi-

years the day was observed with great *eclat;* the troops, in parading, "went through the forms practiced on taking possession of the City, maneuvering and firing *feux-de-joie*, &c., as occurred on the evacuation." All shops and business places were closed, artisans and toilers ceased their work, and the streets, decorated with patriotic emblems, and alive with happy people, were given up to gaiety and mirth. To civic and military displays were added sumptuous dinners, and convivial parties, while the schoolboy rejoiced in a holiday; the whole bearing witness to a peoples' gratitude for the deliverance which that memorable day brought them. And boys of older growth may yet recall the simple distich:

"It's Evacuation Day, when the British ran away,
Please, dear Master, give us holiday!"

In the evening every place of amusement was well attended, but none better than Peale's American Museum, because, as duly advertised:—"The Flag hoisted by order of Gen. Washington, on the Battery, the same day the British troops evacuated this city, is displayed in the upper hall, as a sacred memorial of that day." This flag was presented to the museum by the Common Council in 1819. It was raised on the Battery for the last time in 1846, and when the museum was burned the old flag perished!

Well deserves this day not merely a local but a national commemoration; since it inaugurated for the nation an era of freedom, the blessings of which all could not realize, while the chief city and seaport of our country were held by foreign armies.

Another chapter, introducing us to colonial and revolutionary times, will tell more of Capt. Van Arsdale, what he did and endured for his country, and ensure him a grateful remembrance so long as "Evacuation Day" shall cheer us by its annual return.

---

ness and in the Veteran Corps, gave him the best means of knowing the common belief on that subject, and he said it was "a fact understood and admitted by the members of the Veteran Corps, who used often to speak of it." Capt. George W. Chapman, of the Veteran Corps, then 84 years of age, informed me, in 1845, that he commanded the Corps when Van Arsdale joined it, and that the fact ascribed to the latter was well known to the members of the Corps, and never disputed. John Nixon, a reliable witness, said to me, in 1844, that he saw the ascent, &c., "by *a short thickset man* in sailor's dress," and that *ten years later* (1793) he became acquainted with Van Arsdale, and then learned that '*he was the person who tore down the British flag, in* 1783." Gen. Jeremiah Johnson informed me, in 1846, that he "saw the sailor, in ordinary round jacket and seaman's dress, *shin up* the flagstaff; *a middling sized man*, well proportioned." Major Jonathan Lawrence, who was present, said "a *sailor* mounted the flagstaff, with fresh halyards, rigged it and hoisted the American flag."

CHAPTER II.

THE real conservators of the rights of mankind have rarely been found among the rich or titled aristocracy. They belong to the more ingenuous, sympathetic, and virtuous middle class of society, so called. This is not the less true because of the notable exceptions, where the endowments of wealth, rank, and influence, have added lustre to the names of some of earth's best benefactors. The fact must remain that the bone and sinew of a nation, and in which consists its safety in peace, and its defense in war, are its hardy yeoman who guide the plow, or wield the axe, or ply the anvil; and without whose practical ideas and well-directed energies, no community could protect itself, or make any real advancement. It was most fortunate that the founders of this nation were so largely of this sterling class; the architects of their own fortunes, no labor, no difficulties or dangers appalled them; the very men were they, to break by stalwart blows the fetters which despotism was fast riveting upon them.

Such was Captain John Van Arsdale, in the essentials of his character. It chafed his young, free spirit to see his country, the home of his ancestors for a century before his birth, bleeding under the iron hand of tyranny, and invoking the sturdy and the brave to come forth and strike the blow for freedom. He was one of the first to heed that call, and to fearlessly enter the lists; nor ceased to battle manfully till our independence was achieved! If honest, unswerving patriotism, standing the triple test of manifold hardships and dangers, long and cruel imprisonment and years of arduous, poorly-requited service, should entitle one to the love and gratitude of his country; then let such honor be awarded to the subject of this sketch, and the power of his example tell upon all those who may read it.

John Van Arsdale was the son of John and Deborah Van Arsdale, and was born in the town of Cornwall (then a part of Goshen), Orange County, N. Y., on Monday, January 5th, 1756.* His ancestors for four generations in this country, as mentioned in the records of their times, were men of intelligence and virtue, honored and trusted in the communities in which they lived, and on whom, as God-fearing men, rested the mantles of their fathers who had battled for their faith in the wars of the Netherlands. His grandsire, Stoffel Van Arsdalen (for so he and his Dutch

---

* ARSDALE was formerly pronounced as if written *aurs-daul;* hence the various modes of spelling it to express the Dutch pronunciation by English letters, as *Osdoll,* etc. But the growing disposition to correct such departures by resuming the original form of surnames, leads us to hope for a reformation in this case also, especially as a large part of the family have held to the form which early obtained.

progenitors wrote the name), had removed from Gravesend, Long Island, to Somerset County, New Jersey, in the second decade of that century, and eventually purchased a farm of two hundred acres in Franklin township, where he lived, zealously devoted to the church, and highly esteemed, till his death near the beginning of the Revolution.* He married Magdalena, daughter of Okie Van Hengelen, and had several children, of whom, John, born 1722, and Cornelius, born 1729, removed to the County of Orange, aforesaid.† John, by trade a millwright, was engaged by Mr. Tunis Van Pelt to build a grist mill on Murderer's Creek, so called from an Indian tragedy of earlier times ; and from which name softened to Murdner, in common usage, came the modern Moodna. While so occupied, and sharing the hospitalities of Mr. Van Pelt's house, he wooed and married his daughter, Deborah, in 1744. Associating with his father-in-law in the milling

---

* SIMON JANSEN VAN ARSDALEN, the grandfather of Stoffel, (in English, Christopher,) was the common ancestor of all in this country bearing the name of *Van Arsdale*, or its modification, *Van Osdoll*, which latter preserves the Dutch pronunciation. He was born in Holland in 1629, of an ancient Helvetian family, emigrated to this country in 1653, and settled in Flatlands, L. I., where he married Peternelle, daughter of Claes (or Nicholas) Wyckoff. He acquired property, was a magistrate and repeatedly chosen an elder of the church, and lived to be over four score years of age. He had, besides daughters, two sons, Cornelius and John, both of whom inherited their father's virtues and were prominent in civil and church affairs. Each of these had six sons (Cornelius had *Derick, John, Simon, Philip, Abraham* and *Jacobus* or *James ;* and John had *Simon, Stoffel, Nicholas, Jurian,* or *Uriah, John* and *Cornelius*), most of whom (except Nicholas who lived in Jamaica, L. I.,) settled about the Raritan in New Jersey, whence some removed into Pennsylvania ; they were as a family, remarkably attached to the church and to the elder Frelinghuysens. John, first named, married, 1695, Lammetie, daughter of Stoffel Probasko, lived for some years in Gravesend, but died in the town of Jamaica, about 1756, and as will be seen was the father of Stoffel, named in the text. The family has been very prolific, and has furnished to society many capable business men, besides physicians, clergymen, bankers, etc. Of these was the late Dr. Peter Van Arsdale, of this city.

† ABENT TEUNISSEN, great grandfather of Magdalena Van Hengelen, came out to this country from Hengelen (now Hengelo), in the County of Zutphen, in 1653, the same year in which Simon Van Arsdale arrived. He was under engagement to Baron Vander Capelle, to cultivate his lands on Staten Island, but was slain in the Indian massacre of 1655. His son Reynier, was the father of Okie Van Hengelen, named in the text, who left descendants in New Jersey, called *Van Anglen*, of whom was Capt. John Van Anglen, of the Revolution.

business, Van Arsdale eventually became proprietor, assisted, we
believe, by his brother Cornelius, who was a miller. Building
up a large trade, he also became known for his private virtues
and public spirit. A lieutenant's commission (in which he is
styled "of Ulster County, Gentleman"), under Capt. Thomas
Ellison, and dated October 10th, 1754, is now in the writer's possession. But misfortune, the loss of a vessel sent to the Bay of
Honduras laden with flour, and where it was to ship a cargo of
logwood, led him to give up the business and remove to New
York, where he took charge of the Prison in the old City Hall, in
Wall street, which was deemed a post of great responsibility. It
was soon after this change that John, the subject of our sketch,
was born, at Mr. Van Pelt's residence, at Moodna, where his
mother had either remained, or was then making a visit. About
six weeks thereafter, having come to the city, with her infant, she
sickened and died of the small pox. After four years (in 1760),
Mr. Van Arsdale married Catherine, daughter of James Mills,
deputy-sheriff of New York. Ten years later, weary of his charge,
then at the New Jail, built in 1757-9 (the Provost of the Revolution, and now the Hall of Records); he resigned it, bought a
schooner, and engaged in the more congenial pursuit of market-
ing produce.

The Revolution coming on, Capt. Van Arsdale entered with his
vessel into the American service, supplied our army at New York
with fuel brought from Hackensack (the Asia man-of-war once
taking his wood and paying him in continental bills), and afterwards helped to sink the *chevaux-de-frize* in the Hudson, opposite
Fort Washington. In this arduous work he was aided by his son
John, then lately returned from the Canada expedition. The day
the enemy entered the City he conveyed his family to his vessel
at Stryker's Bay, and, crowded with fugitives, made good his
escape up the Hudson to Murdner's Creek. Here his companion,
who had borne him eleven children, died in 1779; but he survived
not only to witness the war brought to a happy close, but long
enough to see much of the waste repaired, and the greatness of
his country assured. Respected and beloved for his amiable
qualities and exemplary christian character, Capt. Van Arsdale,
the elder, died in 1798 at the residence of his son-in-law, Mr.
William Sherwood, at " The Creek."

The junior Van Arsdale would have been unworthy his honest
ancestry had he not possessed in a good degree the same stability
of character. Bereft of a mother's love at so early an age, John
was tenderly reared at his grandfather Van Pelt's till his father
married again. Then New York became his home for ten years
or more, during which time his playground was the Green (now
City Hall Park) with the fields adjacent to the New Jail, of which

his father still had the custody. The times were turbulent, and many stirring scenes passed under his boyish eyes. One was the Soldiers' Riot, in 1764, when the jail was assaulted and broken into by a party of riotous soldiers, with design to release a prisoner, and in which Mr. Mills, in resisting them, was rudely handled and wounded. And the gatherings, hardly less tumultuous, of the " Sons of Liberty " to oppose the Stamp Act, or celebrate its repeal, by raising liberty poles, which were several times cut down and replaced, all serving to implant in his young mind an abhorrence of foreign rule, with the germs of that patriotism which matured as he grew in years.* But an elder brother Tunis (his only own brother living, save Christopher, a brassfounder, who died, unmarried, in the West Indies in 1773), having served an apprenticeship with Fronce Mandeville, of Moodna, blacksmith, married, in 1771, Jennie Wear, of the town of Montgomery, and the next spring began married life on a farm of eighty acres, which he had purchased, lying in that part of Hanover Precinct (now Montgomery) called Neelytown. Much attached to Tunis, John thereafter spent several years with him, attending school.

But now the growing controversy between the Colonies and the mother country had ripened into actual hostilities; the first aggressive movement in which this Colony took part being the expedition against Canada, planned in the summer of 1775. It fired young Van Arsdale's patriotism, and about August 25th he enlisted under Capt. Jacobus Wynkoop, of the Fourth New York Regiment, James Holmes being the colonel and Philip Van Cortlandt the lieutenant-colonel. These forces, proceeding up the Hudson, entered Canada by way of lakes George and Champlain; part of the Fourth Regiment, under Major Barnabas Tuthill, taking part in the brilliant assault upon Quebec, December 31st, but unsuccessful, and fatal to the gallant leader, General Montgomery, and numbers of his men. On their way to Quebec, and especially in crossing the lakes on the ice, Van Arsdale and his comrades suffered so intensely from the extreme cold that the hardships and incidents of this, his first campaign, remained fresh in his memory even till old age. Van Arsdale having "served his time out in the year's service, returned to New York," where the Americans were

---

* Opposite the jail stood, in those days, a public whipping post, stocks, etc., the terror of law-breakers, and by which lesser crimes were expiated. The late Abraham Van Arsdale, born the year of the Soldiers' Riot (and old enough to fly his kite, as he did, from the roof of the prison, while his father kept it), well remembered these instruments of justice, and informed me that he had seen gallows erected and persons executed, in front of the jail. They then hung for stealing!

concentrating troops, in order to oppose the royal forces expected from Europe. Here he assisted his father on board the schooner in sinking the obstructions in the Hudson, as before noticed, and when the enemy captured the city, accompanied him to Orange County. It was on Sept. 16th, 1776, that the British forces landed at Kip's Bay, on the east side of the island, three miles out of the city. A great many of the citizens who were friends of their country, made a precipitate flight, and the roads were lined with vehicles of every kind, removing furniture, etc. The elder Van Arsdale, with difficulty, and only by paying down $200, got the use of a horse and wagon to take his family and effects from his house to the schooner. lying in Stryker's Bay. While drawing a load, a spent cannon ball knocked off one of the wagon wheels, at which his little son Cornelius, but eight years old, was so frightened that he never forgot it. The schooner was crowded to excess with citizens and their families, all eager to get away, and for fear they might sink her, Capt. Van Arsdale was obliged to turn off some who applied for a passage. They left deeply loaded, and in their haste were obliged to take with them a lot of military stores which were on board. Arriving at Murdner's Creek, John, at his father's request, and taking his brother Abraham, set out afoot for Neelytown, to inform their brother Tunis of their arrival. The journey of twelve miles seemed short, and ere long the well-known farmhouse hove in sight, seated a little way back, and to which led a lane between rows of young cherry trees, and near it on the road the low, dusky smith-shop, with its *debris* of cinders, old wheeltires and broken iron-work strewn about. Entering, as Tunis, with his back towards them, stood at the forge heating his iron, and his assistant, Aleck Bodle, lazily blowing the bellows, the first surprize was only surpassed, when after hearty greetings, they imparted the startling news of the capture of New York by the British, and that their father, having barely escaped with his vessel, had arrived at the Creek. At once out went the fire, and out went Tunis also to harness his horses, in order to go and bring up the rest of the family; but on second thought, as the day was far spent, he concluded to await the morrow. The next day there was a joyous reunion at the farm-house, but tempered with many sad comments upon the doleful situation.

John spent the winter with his brother Tunis, aiding in farm work and at the forge; he had just reached his majority, and found congenial spirits in Alexander Bodle and Joseph Elder, then serving apprenticeships with Tunis, and afterwards much respected residents of Orange County. Around the evening fireside they indulged in many a joke, when laughter made the welkin ring, or behind the well-fed pacer, were borne in the clumsy box sled, with the gingle of merry bells, to the rustic frolic ; but the bounds of decorum were never exceeded, and lips which could tell all about it, bore us pleasing witness to Van Arsdale's correct habits and deportment at a stage of life so beset with syren snares for the unwary, and which commonly moulds the character.

But nevertheless the winter was one of great military activity, especially among the organized militia of Orange County, in which (in the town of New Windsor) was the sub-district of Little Britain, the home of the Clintons ;* the menacing attitude of the enemy under Lord Howe, who had approached as near as Hackensack, and the protection of the passes of the Highlands, requiring frequent calls upon the yeomanry to take the field. The inhabitants of Hanover Precinct, which precinct joined on New Windsor, had from the first shown great spirit ; their Association, dated May 8th, 1775, in which they pledge their support to the Continental Congress, &c., in resisting "the several arbitrary and oppressive acts of the British Parliaments," and "in the most solemn manner resolve never to become slaves," is signed first by Dr. Charles Clinton and presents 342 names. The Precinct in the winter of 1776-7, contained four militia companies, under Captains Matthew Felter, James Milliken, Hendrick Van Keuren and James McBride, and these were attached to a regiment of which that sterling patriot, James McClaughry, of Little Britain, brother in law to the Clintons, was lieutenant colonel commandant.† Tunis and John Van Arsdale lived in Capt. Van Keuren's beat. The Captain was a veteran of the last French war, and it gave him prestige, in the command to which he had been recently promoted. He had "warmly espoused the cause of his country, and evinced unshaken firmness throughout the whole of the contest." Col. McClaughry had taken the field with his regiment early in the winter, proceeding down into Jersey, and of which, on his return, Jan. 1st, he gave a humorous account to Gen. Clinton ; but though highly probable, we have no positive evidence that John Van Arsdale went into actual service till the spring opened.

Forts Montgomery and Clinton, begun in 1775, stood on the west side of the Hudson, opposite Anthony's Nose, at a very important pass, where the river was narrow, easily obstructed, and

---

* To avoid confusion, we speak here and elsewhere of Orange County as now organized. Previous to 1798, it embraced the present Rockland County, while the town of New Windsor, and all those towns lying to the north of a line running west from the southern boundary of New Windsor belonged to Ulster County. Of course, Little Britain, and the Precinct of Hanover were then in Ulster.

† James Clinton had been colonel of this regiment, till appointed a brigadier general.

from the elevation which the forts occupied, was commanded a great distance up and down. Fort Clinton was below Fort Montgoméry, distant only about six hundred yards, the Poplopen Kill running through a ravine between them ; the fortress was small, but [more complete than Fort Montgomery, and stood at a greater elevation, being 23 feet the highest, and 123 feet above the river. These posts were distant (southeast) from the Clinton mansion only about sixteen miles. The two fortresses required a thousand men for their proper defense, but till early in 1777, had usually been in charge of a very small force under Gen. James Clinton. The time of these soldiers expiring on the last day of March, Col. Lewis Dubois, with the Fifth New York Regiment was sent to garrison Fort Montgomery.

A meeting of the field officers of Orange and Ulster, was held at Mrs. Falls' in Little Britain, March 31st, 1777, pursuant to a resolve of the New York Convention empowering General George Clinton, lately appointed commandant of the forts in the High-lands, to call out the militia " to defend this State against the incursions of our implacable enemies, and reinforce the garri-sons of Fort Montgomery, defend the post of Sidnam's Bridge (near Hackensack), and afford protection to the distressed inhabit-ants." It was there resolved, with great spirit, to call one-third of each of the several regiments into actual service, to the num-ber of 1,200, and to form them into three temporary regiments, of which two should garrison Fort Montgomery, under Colonel Levi Pawling (with Lt. Col. McClaughry), and Col. Johannes Snyder. As the men were raised they were to march in detach-ments to that post, and were to serve till August 1st, and receive continental pay and rations. Each captain was forthwith direct-ed to raise his quota, and "in the most just and equitable manner."

John Van Arsdale was among those chosen from his beat, and sometime in April, borrowing from his brother an old but trusty musket, proceeded to Fort Montgomery. Being of a resolute, active temperament, with a knowledge of tactics, and an aptness to command, he was made a corporal ; an evidence of the good opinion entertained of him by his officers, flattering to one of his years. It was also in his favor that he was a good penman, and had acquired a fair English education for the times. Drilling his squad, placing and relieving the guards, and other daily routine duty, gave our young corporal enough to do, while the courts for the trial of some notorious tories, held at that post, during the spring and summer, added to frequent alarms due to indications that the enemy from below meditated an attack upon the forts, kept everything lively. On

July 2nd, Gen. Clinton, upon a hint from Washington that Lord Howe, in order to favor Burgoyne, might attempt to seize the passes of the **Highlands, and "make him a very hasty** visit," with which view, accounts given **by deserters from New** York coincided; immediately repaired **to Fort** Montgomery, after first ordering to that post the full **regiment** of Col. McClaughry, with those of Colonels William Allison, Jesse Woodhull, **and** Jonathan Hasbrouck. The militia came in with great alacrity, almost to a man. But ten days passed without a sign of the enemy. Parties went daily on the Dunderbergh (Thunder Mountain) **to** look down the river, but could not see a single vessel; then, **as** usual, when there was **no** immediate prospect of any thing **to do, the** transient **militia** became uneasy, and were allowed to go home **in the belief** that they would turn out more cheerfully the next time.

But as the term of service of those called out in April expired on August 1st, on that date another call was made by Gov. Clinton on the respective regiments, to make up eight companies, by ballot or other equitable mode, and to march with due expedition to Fort Montgomery, and there put themselves under command of Colonel Allison, with McClaughry as his Lieutenant Colonel. They were to draw continental pay, etc, In this instance no immediate danger being apprehended, the militia did not respond very promptly, although much needed to replace part of the continental force which had been withdrawn for other service. Again, on August 5th, Clinton, by virtue of threatening news from Gen. Washington, directed Allison and McClaughry to march all the militia to Fort Montgomery, except the frontier companies, which were to be left for home protection. But repeated orders to urge them forward were but partially successful. September closed, the quotas were far from complete, orders then issued by Allison, McClaughry, and Hasbrouck (by direction of Clinton) for half their regiments to repair to Fort Montgomery were but slowly complied with, and the delay was fatal! Van Arsdale had re-enlisted and held his former position. It was at this time that he made the acquaintance of Elnathan Sears, and which ripened into friendship under very trying circumstances.

Forts Montgomery and Clinton at this date mounted thirty-two cannon, rating from 6 to 32 pounders. The garrison consisted of two companies of Col. John Lamb's artillery, under Capts. Andrew Moodie and Jonathan Brown (one in each fort) and parts of the regiments of Cols. Dubois, Allison, Hasbrouck, Woodhull and McClaughry with a very few from other regiments. Thus matters stood on Sunday, October 5th, 1777.

Hark! what bustling haste—of people running to and fro,—has suddenly disturbed the Sabbath evening's repose at Neelytown? Tidings have just reached them that the enemy's vessels are ascending the Hudson with the obvious design of attacking Fort Montgomery and the neighboring posts. The orders are for every man able to shoulder a musket to hasten to their assistance! This was grave intelligence for the inmates at the Van Arsdale home (and which may serve to represent many others), but the call of duty could not be disregarded. For most of the night the good wife was occupied in baking and putting up provisions for Tunis and his two apprentices to take with them, while these were as busy cleaning their muskets, moulding bullets, etc., that naught might be wanting for the stern business before them. Towards morning, taking one or two hours rest, they arose, equipped themselves, and made ready for the journey to the fort, which was full twenty miles distant. As the parting moment had come, the kind father kissed his three little ones tenderly, then uttered in the ear of his sorrowing Jennie the sad good-bye, and with the others hastened from the house, his wife attending him to the road, and weeping bitterly for she understood but too well that it might be the final parting. Her longing eyes followed them till they disappeared beyond an intervening hill. "Oh!" said she to the writer more than sixty years afterwards, as she related these facts, her eyes even then suffused with tears, "You may *read* of these things, but you can never *feel* them as I did. I wept much during those seven years."

During the day, those whose kinsmen had gone to the battle met here and there in little bands to condole with each other, and talk over the unhappy situation. Later, the boom of distant artillery awakened their worst fears, for now were they sure that those dear to them were engaged in a mortal conflict with the enemy. The shades of evening closing around, brought no relief to their burdened hearts; but, on the contrary, the most torturing suspense as to the issue of the battle. To make the situation more depressing, there came on a cold rain, and the dreariness without was a fit index of the desolate hearts within. At a late hour Mrs. Van Arsdale retired to her sleepless pillow; but her case found its counterpart in many an anxious household over a large section of country.

At length morning broke upon that unhappy neighborhood, and with it came persons from the battle bringing the appalling news that the Americans had been defeated, and many of them slain, or made prisoners, and that the enemy were in full possession of the forts. Then other parties arrived whose woe-stricken faces only confirmed the sad intelligence. Soon anxious inquiries sped from house to house where any lived who had escaped from the slaughter, to learn about this one and that, who had gone to the battle, but had not returned. Jennie could get no tidings of her husband, though she spent the greater part of the day in watching on the road, and several times even fancied that she saw him coming ; but alas ! only to find it a delusion. It added to her fears for her husband, when a neighbor named Monell, at whose house she called, met her with the sorrowful news that his brother, Robert Monell, first lieutenant in Capt. Van Keuren's company, had been killed in the battle. At length the apprentices arrived, their faces begrimed with powder, and one of them crying for his brother, who had been shot down by his side, and died instantly. * The other, who was Joseph Elder, before spoken of, a young man of giant frame, had narrowly escaped death, having his hat and jacket pierced with bullets in the engagement ! But having been separated from Mr. Van Arsdale, they had not seen him since the battle, and so were ignorant as to his fate. The wretched woman was in dispair ; many of her neighbors had now returned and the prolonged absence of her Tunis seemed to forbode that he had either been killed or captured by the enemy. But now still others arrive, and she is led from their statements, to hope that Tunis has escaped, and is making his way homeward through the mountains. Her heart leaps with joy, and she returns to the house, and even indulges a laugh as her eye gets a sight of the mush kettle still hanging on the trammel, as she placed it there in the morning ; no meal stirred in, and she having eaten nothing the whole day. Towards night Tunis arrived, on horseback, with his brother-in-law William Wear, who at Jennie's request, had gone out some distance to look for him. † He was fast asleep from exhaustion when they reached the house, (Wear behind him and holding him on the horse), and his face so

---

* Believed to have been James Thompson, whose brother John was killed at Fort Montgomery. Others slain in McClaughry's regiment were *Capts.* James Milliken and Jacobus Roosa, *Lieut.* Nathaniel Milliken, and *Privates* Theophilus Corwin, David Benson, James Gage, David Halliday, etc.

† The WEARS, respectable Protestants from the north of Ireland, were noted for longevity. William Wear, their ancestor, dying, his widow with two children, William and Jennie, emigrated to Pennsylvania in 1749, and thence in 1760 to the town of Montgomery. Mrs. Wear died at her daughter's house December 3, 1803, aged 92 years. Her son William, named in the text, resided near Orange Lake, had a numerous family, and attained the age of 97 years. He died November 7, 1828, and was ancestor of William Wear, Esq. Mrs. Van Arsdale was born March 31, 1746, as maintained by her brother, who was much the oldest, and hence was in her 100th year at her decease, September 17, 1845. Her husband, Tunis, died April 9, 1813, aged 67 years. This worthy pair united with the Walkill Church in 1782. Mrs. V. was a woman of remarkable energy, and retained her faculties till the last, almost perfectly. Her memory extended back to the closing events in the life of Steffel Van Arsdale, her husband's grandfather, and she lived to see his descendants of the sixth generation.

blackened with powder that his wife hardly knew **him**. **He was much** depressed in spirits, but grateful to God who **had preserved and** restored him to his family and friends. That evening brought **in his** captain, Van Keuren, who for some cause was not in the fight, with his minister, Rev. Andrew King, and **many** other neighbors—a house full,—some to congratulate Van Arsdale **on** his escape, others, with anxious **faces to** inquire after **missing** friends, and others still to learn **the** particulars of the **battle**. The account he **gave of** what happened after **leaving home for the** scene **of** conflict, was briefly **as** follows :

A walk of several hours brought **them to** a little **stream at the** foot of the hill upon which **Fort Montgomery stood, and where** they had **intended to stop and eat their dinner; but hearing a great deal of noise and bustle in the fort, they only took a drink from the brook, and hastened up into the** works, **when they soon** learned **that a large body of the enemy** had landed **below the** Dunderbergh, **and were advancing by a** circuitous **route to attack the fort in the rear.** About the middle of the afternoon **the Brit-ish columns appeared, and pressed on** to the assault **with bayo-nets fixed.** But our men poured **down upon them such a destruc-**tive fire of bullets and grape shot **that they fell in heaps, and were** kept at bay till night-fall, when **our folks, being worn out by con-**tinued fighting, and overpowered **by numbers, were obliged to** give way. Then Gov. Clinton told them to escape **for their lives,** when many fought their way out, **or** scrambled over **the wall,** and so got away. It must have **fared** badly with the rest, **as the** enemy after entering the fort continued to **stab,** knock down and **kill our** soldiers without pity. **Favored** by the darkness, Tunis attempted **to** escape through one of **the entrances, though it was** nearly blocked **up** by the assailing column, and **the heaps of** killed and **wounded ;** but presently, **as an** English **soldier held a** militiaman **bayoneted** against the wall, **Tunis, stooping down,** slipped **between the Briton's legs, and** escaped around **the fort** toward **the river.** He said he had gone but a little way, **when a** cry **of distress, evidently from a young person,** arrested his atten-tion. A poor **boy, in making his escape, had fallen into a crevice** in the rocks, and was unable to extricate himself. **Tunis, at no** little **risk,** crept down **to where** the lad **was and drew** him **out,** but in doing so hurt himself quite badly, by scraping one of his legs on a sharp rock. He then gained the river and found a skiff, in which he and two or three others crossed over. Then a party **of** them travelled in Indian file, through the darkness and cold drizzling rain, stopping once **at the** house of a friendly farmer, where they got some food, and as the day broke entered Fishkill; whence they crossed to New Windsor, and there met Gov. Clinton and **many more who** had made good their escape. All felt greatly dispirited, but the **Governor tried to cheer** them, remarking: "Well, my boys, **we've been** badly **beaten this** time, but have courage, the next time **the day may be ours."** Without much delay **Mr.** Van Arsdale set out for home, as fast **as his** lameness admitted of, knowing how great anxiety would be felt on his account. But of **his** brother John; he had no knowledge **of what** had befallen him, and indulged the worst fears as to his fate.

Such in brief was Van Arsdale's account of that sanguinary affair, divested of many little particulars of the battle and its **sequel.** But **his** limited observation could include but a small part **of** what **passed** on that most eventful day, **as** we **are now** able **to gather it** from many sources.

With a view to coöperate with General Burgoyne, who had invaded **the State from the north,** Lieutenant-General Sir Henry Clinton, **having a force of about 3,000 men,** sailed from New York **on the** 4th of October, **with** the design of reducing the forts in the Highlands, **and, if** possible, **open** communication with Burgoyne's army. **The same** night their advance as far as Tarrytown **was** known at Fort **Montgomery,** and that they had landed a large **force at** that place. **The next** morning (Sunday) advices **were received** that **they had reached** King's Ferry, connecting **Verplank's** and Stony Point. **That** afternoon they landed a large **body of men** on the east side **of the river, to** divert attention from **the real** point of attack, but they re-embarked in **the** night. An extract from Sir Henry Clinton's report to **General Howe,** dated Fort Montgomery, October 9th, will begin **at this** point, **and form** a proper introduction to **our side** of **the story. Says** he:

"**At** day-break on **the 6th** the **troops** disembarked at Stony **Point.** The *avant-garde* of 500 regulars and **400** provincials,* commanded by Lieut.-Col. Campbell, **with** Col. Robinson, of the provincials, under him, began its march **to** occupy the pass of **Thunder-hill (Dunderbergh).** This *avant-garde,* after it had **passed that mountain, was to proceed** by a detour of seven miles round **the hill (called Bear Hill), and** *deboucher* in the rear of Fort Montgomery; while Gen. Vaughan, with 1200 men,† was to continue his march towards Fort Clinton, covering the corps under Lieut.-Col. Campbell, **and** *à portée* to coöperate, by attacking Fort Clinton, **or, in** case of misfortune, to favor the retreat. Major-Gen. Tryon, **with** the remainder, being the rear guard,‡ to

---

* The 52d and 27th Regiments, the Royal American Regiment, Col. Beverly Robinson, the New York Volunteers, Major Grant, and Emerick's Provincial Chasseurs.

† Grenadiers and Light Infantry, the 26th and 63d Regiments, one company of the 71st Highlanders, one troop of dismounted dragoons, and Hessian Chasseurs.

‡ The Royal Fusileers and **Hessian** Regiment of Trumback.

leave a battalion at the pass of Thunder-hill, to open our communication with the fleet.

"Your Excellency recollecting the many, and I may say extraordinary difficulties of this march over the mountains, every natural obstruction, and all that art could invent to add to them, will not be surprised that the corps intended to attack Fort Montgomery in the rear, could not get to its ground before five o'clock; about which time I ordered Gen. Vaughan's corps, *à portée*, to begin the attack on Fort Clinton, to push, if possible, and dislodge the enemy from their advanced station behind a stone breastwork, having in front for half a mile a most impenetrable abatis. This the General, by his good disposition, obliged the enemy to quit, though supported by cannon; got possession of the wall, and there waited the motion of the coöperating troops,—when I joined him, and soon afterwards heard Lieut. Col. Campbell begin the attack. I chose to wait a favorable moment before I ordered the attack on the side of Fort Clinton, which was a circular height, defended by a line for musketry, with a barbet-battery in the centre, of three guns, and flanked by two redoubts; the approaches to it through a continued abatis of four hundred yards, defensive every inch, and exposed to the fire of ten pieces of cannon. As the night was approaching, I determined to seize the first favorable instant. A brisk attack on the Fort Montgomery side, the gallies with their oars approaching, firing and even striking the fort, the men-of-war at that moment appearing, crowding all sail to support us, the extreme ardor of the troops, in short, all determined me to order the attack; Gen. Vaughan's spirited behavior and good conduct did the rest. Having no time to lose, I particularly ordered that not a shot should be fired; in this I was strictly obeyed, and both redoubts, &c., were stormed.* Gen. Tryon advanced with one battalion to support Gen. Vaughan, in case it might be necessary, and he arrived in time to join in the cry of victory!

"Trumbach's Regiment was posted at the stone wall to cover our retreat, in case of misfortune. The night being dark, it was near eight o'clock before we could be certain of the success of the attack against Fort Montgomery, which we afterwards found had succeeded at the same instant that of Fort Clinton did; and *that* by the excellent disposition of Lieut. Col. Campbell, who was unfortunately killed on the first attack, but was seconded by Col. Robinson, of the loyal American Regiment, by whose knowledge of the country I was much aided in forming my plan, and

---

* This refers only to the final assault; the enemy fired upon our people both in the preliminary skirmishes and after they were masters of the forts. J. R.

to whose spirited **conduct in the execution** of it, I impute in a great measure **the success of the** enterprise."

From this official account **by the** British commander, we shall better understand the statements (including **Gov. Clinton's report**) left us by the brave defenders of the two beleaguered fortressess; and which will properly begin **upon the** day preceding **the** battle.

On Sunday **night** Gov. Clinton, who had just arrived and taken command at **Fort** Montgomery, (the defense of Fort Clinton being **intrusted to** his brother Gen. James Clinton), sent out a **party of** about 100 men under Major Samuel Logan of the 5th, **or Dubois's** regiment, across the Dunderbergh to watch the **motions of** the enemy. The party returned in the morning and **reported that** they had seen about forty boats full of men land **below the** Dunderbergh. **The** real intention **of the** enemy was **now** apparent. Hereupon **the Governor** sent out another party **of** observation, **consisting of 30 men, under Lieut.** Paton Jackson **(5th** regiment) **who took the road that** led to Haverstraw; **when** at about **ten o'clock in the forenoon,** having reached a **point** some **two miles and a half below Fort** Montgomery, **they** suddenly **came upon a concealed** party **of the enemy, within** five rods **distant, who ordered them** to club **their** muskets **and** surrender **themselves prisoners.** They made **no answer,** but **fired** upon the enemy and hastily retreated. **The fire was returned and our people were pursued** half a mile; **but** they got off without **losing a man, and** retired **into** Fort Clinton. **Soon** after, intelligence was received at Fort Montgomery **that the enemy were advancing on** the **west side of** Bear Hill **to attack** that work in the **rear. Upon** this **Gov. Clinton immediately sent out** 100 men **under Lieut. Col. Jacobus Bruyn (5th regiment)** and Lieut. Col. **McClaughry,** to take the road around **Bear Hill** to meet the approaching enemy; and at the same time dispatched another party **of 60 men, of** Lamb's Artillery, with a brass field piece, to occu**py a commanding** eminence on the **road that** diverged westerly to **Orange Furnace, or Forest of Dean. They** were not long out, **before both** parties **were** attacked, about two o'clock in the afternoon, by the **enemy in** full force. The party under Cols. Bruyn and McClaughry, **fell in with them two** miles from the fort, when the enemy hailing **McClaughry,** who took the **lead, inquired how many men** he had. "**Ten to your** one, d——n you," **replied** the **undaunted colonel. But the enemy being** so superior **in** numbers, **our** people **had to retreat, as of course they had expected,** yet keeping up **a galling fusilade upon the foe.** While doing so, the ground being **very** rough **and in** places **steep,** Capt. James Humphrey, McClaughry's **brother in law, lost** his **gun (for** then the American captains carried both a gun and sword), or as others say, and which seems most correct, had it broken by a shot from the enemy. In this dilemma he asked McClaughry what he should do. "Throw stones like the devil," replied the latter in thunder tones! The party on the Furnace road were strengthened to upwards of an hundred, and kept their field piece playing lively upon the cautiously advancing foe, doing great execution, till the cannoniers were driven off with the bayonet, the enemy almost surrounding them. But spiking the gun, they retreated in good order to a twelve pounder, which by the Governor's direction had been placed to cover them, and also keeping up the engagement with small arms, till most of them got within the breastwork of the fort. The late Lieut. Timothy Mix, of Lamb's Artillery, and who died at New Haven in 1824, aged 85 years, was of this party. · While in the act of firing the cannon his right hand was disabled by a musket shot. Instantly seizing the match with his left, he touched off the piece!

Clinton immediately posted his men in the most advantageous manner for defending the works, and before many minutes the enemy, advancing in several columns, reached the walls and invested them on every side where possible to do so. Cannon planted at the entrances mowed them down as they ascended the hill, but the breach was immediately closed up, and they pressed on to the assault. The attack now became general on both forts, and was kept up incessantly for some time; though the smallness of our numbers (about 500, in both forts), which required every man to be upon continual duty and demanded unremitted exertion, fatigued our people greatly, while the enemy, whose number was thought to be at least 4,000, continued to press us with fresh troops. Yet notwithstanding their utmost efforts, the enemy were many times repulsed and beaten back from our breastworks with great slaughter. Col. Mungo Campbell fell in leading the first attack on Fort Montgomery, his place being taken by Col. Beverly Robinson, of the Loyal Americans. This caused a temporary check. About half-past four, they sent a flag, which Lt.-Col. William Livingston was deputed by the Governor to go out and receive. They demanded a surrender in five minutes, to prevent the effusion of blood, otherwise we should all be put to sword! The gallant young colonel answered, with irony, that he would accept their proposals if *they* meant to surrender, and could assure them good usage; that *we* were determined to defend the fort *to the last extremity!* Then the action was renewed with fresh vigor on both sides; our officers aiding and encouraging their men to every possible effort. Col. McClaughry was one of the most active; full of fire, he fought like a tiger; his white coat was seen, now here, now there, as he kept going about among his men, inspiring them with his own invincible spirit. The conflict went on until the dusk of evening, when the enemy stormed the upper redoubt at Fort Montgomery, which commanded the fort, and after a severe struggle, and overpowering us with numbers, got possession of it, when our men were forced to give way. The first to enter the fort were the New York Volunteers (led by Capt. George Turnbull), a provincial corps, whose commander, Major Grant, was killed before the assault. At the same time they stormed and got possession of Fort Clinton, in which, besides a company of Lamb's Artillery, were none but militia, but who nobly defended it, till they also were obliged to yield to superior force. The garrisons, or as many as could, bound not to surrender, gallantly fought their way out, those of Fort Montgomery retreat-ing across the gully on the north side ; while many others, including Gov. Clinton, escaped over the south breastwork, and making their way down to the water's edge, crossed the river on the boom. The darkness of the evening much favored the escape of our soldiers, as did their knowledge of the various paths in the mountains, and a large number, with nearly all the officers, got away. But many were taken prisoners, and about 100 were slain ; among the latter was a son of Colonel Allison, and Capt. Milliken, of Mc Claughry's regiment (Mr. Sears' captain) ; also James Van Arsdale, of Hanover Precinct, a kinsman of Tunis and John, and a private in Dubois's regiment. John Thompson was killed, who was nearly related to the Clintons, and cousin to William Bodle, Esq., late of Tompkins County, N. Y.* The enemy paid dearly for their conquest, both in officers and men, the total being 41 killed and 142 wounded. Among the officers killed, besides Col. Campbell, Majors Grant and Sill, and Capt. Stewart, was Count

---

* JUDGE BODLE was born only a stone's throw from the Clinton homestead, in Little Britain (being a s cond cousin to the Clintons); but at the time of the battle was a farmer on the Walkill. The distance made him late, and he reached the vicinity of the forts only to learn that the enemy had possession. Next morning, going home, he suddenly met Claudius Smith, the noted Tory robber. They knew each other. Bodle was perplexed, but putting on a bold front, approached Claudius, who seemed very friendly. After inquiring the news from the river, Smith said he had to go away, but added: "Mr. Bodle, you are weary, go to my house yonder and ask my wife for some breakfast, and say that I sent you." Seeming to accept his offer, but suspecting a trick, Bodle steered for home, nor felt quite safe till he reached Chester. Smith was a bold, accomplished villain, a terror to the people of Orange, and whose career of brigandage has all the air of romance. He was finally hung at Goshen, January 22, 1779. Mr. Bodle was one of the citizens who guarded him while in jail. Smith asked him if he would really shoot him, if a rescue were attempted. Bodle said his duty would compel him to it. "Ah! Bodle, I don't believe you," said Smith. See *Eager's Orange County*, for an account of Smith and his gang, made up in part from an article we wrote many years ago for the "True Sun." But not a fact in that article (save the incident above related), came from Judge Bodle, as Mr. Eager assumes.

Grabouski, a Polish nobleman acting as aid-de-camp to Sir Henry Clinton ; and Sir Henry himself narrowly escaped our grape-shot, as also Maj. Gen. John Vaughan, whose horse was shot under him.

Many incidents are related of those who met with hair-breadth escapes. Gen. James Clinton was among the last to leave Fort Clinton, and escaped not until he was severely wounded by the thrust of a bayonet, pursued and fired at by the enemy, and his attending servant killed. He slid down a declivity of one hundred feet to the ravine of the creek which separated the forts, and proceeding cautiously along its bank reached the mountains at a safe distance from the enemy, after having fallen into the stream, by which, the water being cold, the flow of blood from his wound was staunched. The return of light enabled him to find a horse, which took him to his house, in Little Britain, where he arrived about noon, covered with blood, and suffering from a high fever. Capt. William Faulkner, of McClaughry's regiment, had a bayonet driven in his breast with such force that, being unfixed at the same moment, it stuck fast, when he himself drew it out, and threw it back with all his might, and his man fell. The enemy were pressing into the fort, and the captain made his way on the ground by the side of the column and got out. Walking a mile or so he lay down to drink at a brook, the draft stopped the blood, but he was too weak to rise. He "made his peace with God" (to use his own expression), and expected there to die. But a man came along on horseback, who placed him on his horse, and took him to an inn two miles beyond. There he found a dozen of his own men, by whom he was taken to his own house on the Walkill, and he finally recovered.*

When the battle had ended, and the enemy had set a guard, Corporal Van Arsdale, who had shown great spirit in the fight, and was among the last to cease firing, resolved not to be made a prisoner, and managed to escape from the fort ; but he had only gone a short distance when he was shot in the calf of the leg, and seized by a British soldier while in the act of crossing a fence. He was conducted back into the fort, under a torrent of abuse from his captor, who threatened to take his life, and he himself expected instant death. His gun was demanded, and when delivered, the barrel was yet so hot from frequent firing that the soldier quickly dropped it, with another imprecation. Then the old musket, its last work so nobly done, was ruthlessly broken to pieces over the rocks. Van Arsdale and

---

* JEPTHA LEE, of Lamb's Artillery, was one of those who escaped out of the fort with General James Clinton. He served with John Van Arsdale, under Capt. Faulkner, in 1779, and died in 1855, at Ulysses, N. Y.

the other prisoners, two hundred and seventy-five in all, including twenty-eight officers, were kept under guard for a day or two at the forts, then put on board the British transports and taken to New York. Forty-four of Van Arsdale's regiment were among them including the brave colonel McClaughry (who was suffering from seven wounds),* and his brother-in-law Capt. Humphrey, of whom it was said by one Van Tuyl (among the last to escape from Fort Montgomery) that, when he left, Humphrey was yet throwing stones! The prisoners, on arriving at New York, October, 10th, were landed, and the privates marched up to Livingston's Sugar House, in Liberty Street, between Nassau and William, and put in custody of Sergeant Woolly; excepting the badly wounded, who were sent to the hospital. The officers, with similar exception, were taken to the old City Hall, whence, two days after, they were marched up to the Provost, and placed in charge of the brutal Cunningham, where they remained till after the surrender of Burgoyne, when, retaliation being feared, nearly all the officers were sent (November 1st) to Long Island, upon parole.† The privates had all been removed from the Sugar House, October 24th, and put on board a prisonship, anchored opposite Governor's Island. Van Arsdale, and his friend Sears, needing surgical aid, were, with others, suffering from their wounds, taken directly to the Presbyterian Church in Beekman Street, known as the "Brick Church," and then used by the enemy as an hospital. Sears had been very badly hurt in the battle. After being shot in the leg, and stabbed in the side by a bayonet, which filled his shoes with blood, he was knocked down with the but of a gun and trampled upon by the invading column. At the hospital, the bullets being extracted

---

* COL. McCLAUGHRY, though a prisoner and sorely wounded, showed the same indomitable spirit as before. Left to suffer three days before his wounds were dressed, in the belief that he could not live, his captors tried to extort information from him, as to our strength. He replied curtly that Washington had a powerful army, and would yet whip them, and he should live to see it! He was soon exchanged, resumed his command and survived the war. He was made an honorary member of the Cincinnati, and lived most respectably upon his farm at Little Britain, till his death in 1790, aged 67 years. He left no children.

GEN. ALLISON, as later styled, was exchanged during the ensuing winter, and took home with him to Gov. Clinton $2,000 in gold, loaned by a good whig on Long Island, to aid the American cause. He died in 1804, at the Drowned Lands, where he resided; leaving a very respectable family and an ample estate. His daughter Sarah married William W. Thompson, and daughter Mary married Dr. William Elmer.

† The exceptions were 'Col. McClaughry, Capt. Humphrey, Lieut. Solomon Pendleton and Ensign John McClaughry, both of Dubois's regiment, and Lieut. John Hunter, of McClaughry's; who were still there Nov 5th.

and their wounds dressed, they began to mend, but only three weeks
and three days elapsed, when they too were sent to the prisonship, and confined between decks. Winter had set in very inclem-
ent, their food was not only stale and unwholesome, but even this
was limited in quantity to two-thirds of a British soldiers when
at sea, which was one-third less than the allowance upon land ;
in consequence of which they suffered everything but death from
hunger and cold. Nor was this the worst. The prisoners, from
these and other causes, became very sickly, and died off in great
numbers. Abel Wells and four others of the Fort Montgomery
party, being tailors, were sent from the prisonship to the Provost,
November 24th, to make clothing for the prisoners there.* They
informed Judge Fell, a prisoner, that their company was then
reduced to one hundred. This mortality would seem to have
been heavy among Col. Dubois's men, very few of whom ever
rejoined their regiment. Van Arsdale was taken sick about the
20th of December, and had the good fortune to be sent to the
hospital, where he had some care, and soon recovered. Shortly
after going there he was joined by Sears, who was in a suffering
and helpless condition, his feet and legs having been badly frozen
in the prisonship. Fortunately Van Arsdale was getting better,
so that he was of great service to his friend, and which also tend-
ed to divert his mind from his own misfortunes. He even begged
"coppers" from the British officers to buy little comforts for
Sears ; but which, had it been for himself, he declared he would
have scorned to do, in any extremity. Sears always held that Van
Arsdale saved his life, and he spoke feelingly of his kindness to
him to the day of his death. Van Arsdale finding his condition
in the hospital much more tolerable, managed to prolong his stay,
by tying up his head and feigning illness when the doctor made his
daily call. The latter would leave him some powders, but only to be
thrown away. This did not long avail him, and when reported well
enough to remove, he was taken back to the prisonship, to en-
dure its indescribable miseries for several weary months. Words
cannot portray the horrors of this prison, which was loathesome

---

* They were, besides Wells, Robert Huston, Francis McBride, and
William Humphrey, of McClaughry's regiment, and John Brooks, of
Woodhull's. Abel Wells sickened and died in the Provost, Dec. 13,
1777. Benjamin Goldsmith and Garret Miller, worthy residents of
Smith's Clove in Orange County, deserve notice in this connection.
Goldsmith had a valuable horse stolen by Claudius Smith's gang, and
some of his neighbors sustained similar losses. Finally a party went
out in pursuit of the robbers, but some, including Goldsmith and Miller,
fell into the hands of the British, and were sent to the Provost, where
both died of small'pox, Miller on the memorable 6th of October, and
Goldsmith on the 20th of October, 1777. Goldsmith was the father of
Daniel, who was the father of the present Mr. Daniel Goldsmith, of
Bloomingrove, and of the late David Goldsmith, of Schuyler Co., N. Y.

with filth and vermin, and where to the pangs of hunger anp thirst, were added the alternate extremes of heat and cold. Especially when the hatches were closed, as was always done at night, the heat and stench caused by the feverish breath of hundreds of prisoners became almost suffocating. Consequently dysentery, small-pox and jail fever made fearful ravages. The ghastly faces of the starved and sick, and the pale corpses of the dead, the groans of the dying, the commingled voices of weeping, cursing and praying, joined to the ravings of the delirious; such were the shocking scenes to which Van Arsdale was a witness, and which added to his personal sufferings, made his situation one of the most appalling to be conceived of. Fitly was this dungeon described by one of its inmates as "a little epitome of Hell!" Kept near to starvation, Van Arsdale, when allowed with other prisoners, a few at a time, to go up on the quarter deck, was glad to eat the beans or crusts he skimmed from the swill kept there to feed pigs, that he might partially relieve the knawings of hunger! But we forbear further comment upon a fruitful topic, the cruel treatment of the American prisoners, and which has fixed a stain upon the perpetrators never to be wiped out!

Sears had returned to the prisonship about the last of March, and in the month of May he and Van Arsdale, with other prisoners, were picked out and removed again to the Sugar House. This was probably a step towards an exchange of prisoners, then contemplated, which made it necessary to separate those belonging to the land service from the naval prisoners. The Sugar House, with its five or six low stories, was crammed with American patriots, and the passerby in warm weather could see its little grated windows filled with human faces, trying to catch a breath of the external air! But now a little more lenity seems to have been shown some of the prisoners, perhaps in view of the exchange. Van Arsdale found a friend in his father's cousin, Vincent Day, who had enlisted in Lamb's Artillery, in 1775, but did not go to Canada, and was now regarded as a loyalist. He was permitted to see Van Arsdale, bring him food, etc.,* and a

---

* This kindness was repaid a dozen year later (1790) when Mr. Van Arsdale and his wife took Mr. Day's eight year old motherless daughter to nurture as their own, they having been bereft the year previous of their three young children, though seven more were given them afterwards. And Mary Day, (whose father died Oct. 19, 1802, aged 49), remained with them till her marriage to William Hutchings, the father of Mr. John Hutchings, of Norwalk, Ct. Amiable woman, pure and artless as a child, and to sum up her life in a word, filling her humble sphere with perfect fidelity,—among the happier days of the writer's boyhood were those spent in summer recreations at her modest home at Cow Bay, with the mill pond and Squire Mitchell's old red grist mill, and Uncle Billy's cooperage near it, and around the bluff the broad sandy beach, as rambling ground; your pardon, indulgent reader, if thoughts of the past do force a tear.

next step was to get leave for him to visit his house. This was a most grateful relief; but it being suspected that Van Arsdale meditated an escape (which my informant said was the case), this privilege was cut off, and Day sent to the Provost for his humanity. This incident was related to me by Mr. Abraham Van Arsdale, before mentioned.

Van Arsdale had dragged out some two months of miserable existence in the Sugar House, and in all nine months and a half as a prisoner, when the day of happy deliverance arrived. Gen. Washington had long been trying to effect an exchange of prisoners, but to overcome the scruples of the British commander took months of negotiation. Terms were at length agreed upon by which some six hundred Americans were set at liberty. On July 20th, Van Arsdale was released from his dungeon, and taken with others in a barge down the bay, and *via* the Kills to Elizabethtown Point, where they landed, and were delivered up to Major John Beatty, the American Commissary. In marching from the Point two miles to the village of Elizabethtown, Van Arsdale was obliged to support his friend Sears, who was too feeble to walk alone. Now breathing the air of freedom, they set out together for their homes in Hanover Precinct, where Van Arsdale was heartily greeted by his numerous friends who received him as one risen from the dead, and found a warm welcome in the house of his brother Tunis. Emaciated to a degree, and suffering from scurvy, he was for some time under the doctor's care, but finally regained his health.

A nation's gratitude is the least tribute it can render to its brave soldiers who have fought its battles; but if any class of patriots should be tenderly embalmed in a nation's memory, it is those who, through devotion to country, have languished in prison walls, whether the "Sugar House," or a "Libby!" What firmness, and what consecration to country was required in the Revolutionary prisoners, under the pressure of their sufferings, to spurn the alluring offers frequently made, to entice them into the British service; but so rarely successful. Do not their names deserve to be written in letters of gold, on the proudest obelisk that national gratitude and munificence united could erect?*

---

* LIST OF THE AMERICANS who were made prisoners at Forts Montgomery and Clinton, Oct. 6, 1777.

OFFICERS.

Col. William Allison.
Lt. Col. James McClaughry.
Lt. Col. Jacobus Bruyn.
Lt. Col. William Livingston.
Major Samuel Logan, 5th Regt.

Lieut. Paton Jackson, 5th Regt.
Lieut. John Furman, 5th Regt.
Lieut. Henry Pawling, 5th Regt.
Lieut. Ebenezer Mott, 5th Regt.
*Lieut. Alexander McArthur, 5th Regt.

Van Arsdale's bitter experience **at the hands of** the Britons, had changed his animosity towards **them into** unmitigated hate, and we know that time **but partially overcame it.** So far from

---

Major Stephen Lush, Brig de Major to
G n. G orge Clinton.
Major Daniel Hamil, Brigade Major **to**
Gen. James Clinton.
Major Zachariah Dubois, Woodhull's
Regt.
Capt. Henry **Godwin, 5th** Regt.
Capt. James **Humphrey,** McClaughry's
Regt.
Capt. Lt. Cornelius Swartwout, Lamb's
Artillery.
Capt. Lt. Ephraim Fenno, Lamb's Ar-
tillery.
Lieut. Solomon Pendleton, 5th Regt.

Lieut. Samuel Dodge, 5th **Regt.**
Lieut. John Hunter, **McClaughry's**
Regt.
Lieut. Benjamin **Halstead, Allison's**
Regt.
Lieut. Henry Brewster, Allison's Regt.
En-ign Abraham Leggett, 5th Regt.
Ensign John McClaughry, 5th Regt.
Ensign Henry Swartwout, 5th Regt.
Adj. Dep. Qr. Mr. Gen. Oliver Glean.
Qr. Master Nehemiah Carpenter.
Capt. James Gilliland, Director of Ord-
nance.

PRIVATES AND NON-COMMISSIONED OFFICERS.

5th, or Col. *Dubois's Regiment.*

David McHollister.
Martin Shay.
Jacobus Terbush.
Thaddeus Kennedy.
John McDonald.
John Conklin.
James Montanye.
Henry Ostrander.
Jacobus Logier.
David Bovins.
Vincent Venney.
Jeremiah Dunn.
Robert Patrick.
William Barber.
Benjamin Wiley,
Danford Winchester.
*William Mallen.
Lewis Dixon.
John Ivers.
Nathaniel Otter.
Eliakim Brush.
Robert Gillespie.
Abraham Wright.
Jonathan Hallock.
James Weldon.
Thomas **Tinn.**
Samuel Turner,
Daniel Dominick.
John Witlock.
Jacobus Terwilliger.
James Steel.
Thomas Crispell.
Enas Lent.
Jacobus Lent.
John Albright.
Alexander Ockey.
Thomas Hartwell.
Patrick Dorgan.
Samuel Crosby.
Moses Shall.
John West.
John McIntosh.
Henry Schoonmaker.
Joseph Morgan.
Jonathan Stockham.
Abel Randall
Thomas Kent.
William Banker.
Peter Wells.
Joseph Deneyck.
John Weston.
Michael Burgh.
Thomas Smith.

Thomas Conklin.
Ephraim Adams.
Francis Sears.
Samuel Garrison.
William Willis.
Abraham Jorden.
John Storm.
Thomas McCarty.
Thomas Hendricks.
John Chamberlin.
Zebulon Woodruff.
Paul Keizler.
George Heck.
John Miller.
John Allison,
Samuel Boyd.
William Weaver.
William **Ivery,**
John **Stanley,**
John **Brown.**
George Polton.
*Philip Felix.
Aaron Knapp.
James Mitchell,
John Johnston.
Nehemiah Sniffen.
Solomon Shaw.
James Montieth.
Daniel Lover.
John **Hunt.**
Michael Johnston
Joseph Reeder.
John Price.
Robert Marshall.
Scott Travers.
John Satterly.
James Amerman.
Harman Crum.
Samuel Griffin.
Cornelius Acker.
Jacob Lawrence.
Francis Gaines.
Benjamin Griffin.
Enos Sniffen
Joseph Bolton
James Hannah
William Slott.
Benjamin Chichester
Francis Drake.
Jasper Smith
William Casselton
Edward Allen
William Bard

weaning him from the dangers and hardships of a soldier's life, it only nerved him with courage, and fixed his purpose to re-enter the service, an opportunity for which soon offered.

The frequent atrocities committed by the Indians and Tories upon the settlers on the frontiers, within New York and Pennsylvania, and especially the massacres, the preceding year, at Wyoming and Cherry Valley, led to retributive measures, which took

COL. LAMB'S ARTILLERY

Elijah Petty,
David Clark.
Hull Peck.
William Taylor.
Edward Keen.
Hugh Lindsey.
David Pembroke.
Thomas Griffith,
Robert English.
David Stone.
John Twitchell.
Hugh McCall.
Thaddeus Barnes.

Alexander Moffatt.
David Hanmore.
James Shearer.
William Swan.
John Patterson.
John Nelson
Israel Smith.
Samuel Furman.
Alexander Young.
John Kelly.
Alexander McCoy.
John Gardner.
Timothy Nichols.

COL. ALLISON'S REGIMENT.

Samuel Taylor.
James Bell,
Robert Eaton,
Richard Sheridan.
James Koyl.
*James Lewis.
James Thompson.
Michael Dunning.
James Sawyer.
Joseph Moore.
Jesse Dunning.

Peter Jones.
Uriah Black.
Frederick Nochton.
David Wheeler.
Peter Stage.
Isaac Ketcham.
Henry Brewster.
Frederick Pelliger.
Caleb Ashley.
Timothy Corwin.

COL. McCLAUGHRY'S REGIMENT.

*John McMullen.
Henry Neely.
Robert Henry.
William Scott.
Matthew Dubois.
Francis McBride.
Robert Huston.
Andrew Wilson.
Christopher Sypher.
John Darkis.
William Stinson
William Humphrey
George Humphrey
James Humphrey.
John Carmichel.
John Skinner.
Gerardus Viueger.
Baltus Van Kleek.
Cornelius Slott.
William Howell.
John Hanan.

Robert Barkley.
James Wood.
David Thompson.
Elias Wool.
*Robert Wool.
*Samuel Hodge.
William McMullen.
Isaac Denton.
Moses Cantine.
George Brown.
Elnathan Sears.
Philip Millspaugh.
John Van Arsdale.
George Coleman.
Abel Wells.
Hezekiah Kune.
John Manny.
Isaac Kinbrick
Samuel Fails.
James Miller.

COL. HASBROUCK'S REGIMENT.

George Wilkin.
Cornelius Roosa.
Simon Ostrander.
Zachariah Terwilliger.
John Stevenson.
William Warren.

Benjamin Lawrence.
Cornelius Stevens.
John Bingham.
John Snyder.
Robert Cooper.

the form of an expedition into the Indian country. This expedition was to move in two divisions; one under Major General Sullivan, who was chief in command, to ascend the Susquehanna river from Easton, the other under General James Clinton to descend that river from the Mohawk Valley; and the two meeting at Tioga Point, the united force was to proceed up the Chemung, to give the Indians battle, should they make a stand, or otherwise to burn and lay waste their villages, orchards and crops, thus depriving them of subsistence, and the power to repeat their bloody forays upon the border settlements.

This design was scarcely matured, when our legislature, on March 13th, 1779, ordered the raising of two regiments from the militia, to be called State Levies, for the special defense of the State, and particularly of the frontiers of Orange and Ulster, which were subject to the stealthy attacks of roving Indians, and of Tories disguised as Indians, the fear of which kept the loyal inhabitants in constant alarm, and called for the maintenance of a military guard to prevent their falling a prey to these destroyers in the British interest, or their abandonment of their homes and possessions. One battalion of levies, so raised, was commanded by Lieut.-Col. Albert Pawling, and under whom, in the company of Capt. William Faulkner, our Van Arsdale enlisted on the 10th of May. Governor Clinton had assured Wash-

COL. WOODHULL'S REGIMENT.

John Brooks.
John Lamerey.
Henry Cunningham.
John Crooks.
William Penoyer.
Simon Currens.
Israel Cushman.
Asa Ramsey.
*Joel Curtiss.
Thomas Harten.
Jesse Carpenter.
Benjamin Simmons.
Isaac Cooly.
Joshua Currey.
James Thompson.
Stephen Clark.

James Mitchell.
John Armstrong.
Peter Gillen.
Edward Tomkins
Randle House.
*Christian House.
Isaac Hoffman.

Col. Hammon's, Zachariah Taylor.
Col. Drake's, John Vantassel.
Col. Holme's, Cornelius Cornelius, William Randle.
Col. Ogden's, Thomas Cook.
Col. Antill's, Jonathan Nichols.

CORPS UNKNOWN.

John Donalds.
Joseph Mead.
George Peck.
Jesse Lockwood.

Tobias Lent.
George Depew.
Auris Verplank.
Albert Vantass.

WAGONERS.

John Randle.
Elias Vanvolver.
Samuel Anderson.

*Jacob Morris.
*John Tallow.

N. B.—The ten with a star are named in a list preserved by Col. Wm. Faulkner, but are not in that furnished Gov. Clinton, by Joseph Loring, British Commissary of Prisoners. McArthur returned to his regiment, the other nine are not found again.

ington that Pawling would reinforce Gen. Clinton on his march, and take part in the expedition. But the sudden seizure of Stony Point by the British, May 31st, and a further advance which menaced West Point and obliged Governor Clinton to take the field with all his available force, together with the burning of Minisink by red and white savages under the cruel Brant, and the fatal battle that ensued, July 22d, near the Delaware, in which fell many of the brave yeomen of Orange, made it so unsafe to withdraw the levies from these borders that Governor Clinton expressed a fear that he might not be able to detach them upon the western expedition.

But eventually Col. Pawling, with his battalion, about five hundred men, left Lackawack and Shandaken, on the borders of Ulster, upon the 10th of August. The route lay across the country for a hundred miles, over mountains and rivers, and through dark forests known only to the guides; but it so happened that, added to these obstacles, the rains set in and the rivers became swollen and impassable, except by rafts. This, with the state of his provisions and other considerations, rendered it impracticable for him to proceed, and he reluctantly turned back. He, however, pushed forward a small detachment of sixteen men, under Capt. Abraham Van Aken, either to advise Gen. Clinton of his approach or of his inability to join him; but Van Aken reached Aghquaga, or Anquaga, on the Susquehanna, the day after Clinton had passed, so missed of seeing him; and remaining there some days, as would appear, then returned to camp, where he arrived September 1st. It transpired that Clinton had reached Anquaga on the 14th, and, waiting till the 16th, then sent out Major Church, with the Fourth Pennsylvania Regiment, five or six miles to look for Pawling, but they returned without seeing him, and the next morning Clinton pursued his march. This was a great disappointed to Van Arsdale and others, who were full of ardor to share in the expedition under Sullivan, and our statement must correct the existing belief that Van Arsdale did take part in it, while it explains how he failed of the coveted opportunity.

Major Van Benschoten, with a detachment of the levies, including Van Arsdale and his company, in which he was serving as corporal, proceeded, October 31st, to the camp on the Hudson, and were ordered to Stony Point to augment its garrison. But the winter setting in with severity, the men through anxiety to reach home, began to desert in great numbers, on account of which they were ordered to Poughkeepsie, and set out December 16th. At Fishkill, the next day they were paid off, up to October 31st, the date they arrived in camp. What Capt. Faulkner then paid him was all that Van Arsdale received in lieu of his services, past or subsequent, till after the **war ended.** **He** remained with his company until it was disbanded **on December 25th,** when he was honorably discharged and went home, having acquitted him as " a good soldier " in the estimation of his captain.

He spent the winter at Neelytown, giving spare time to improving his mind **in** some useful studies. It was the famous "**Hard Winter,**" and it made a fearful draft on the woodpile ; taking **the brothers** often to the woods with their axes, to keep up the **supply of** fuel. Snow covered the ground to an average depth of six **feet or more, fences and** roads were obliterated, and travel went **in all** directions over the hard crust. Being difficult if **not dangerous** for **a team,** they drew their **wood** home on **a haud sled.** On **the** melting of the **snow** in the spring, the stumps left were of sufficient **length** to be **used by** Tunis for making fence rails !

A **dark cloud** hung over **our cause** in the **spring of** 1780 ; there were **no funds** with which **to** pay **the army, or** even to supply it with necessary food **and clothing. Pressed** by keenest want, officers **were resigning, large bodies of** soldiers whose time had expired **were leaving, while such as remained were** disheartened, —less **by the remembrance of hardships past, than by** what the future **seemed to forebode. It was under such** discouragements, when

> " Allegiance wand'ring turns astray
> And Faith grows dim for lack of pay."

that **Van Arsdale re-entered the army, to share its fortunes** whatever those **might be. An Act had been passed March 11th,** 1780, **to** raise a body of levies for the defense of the **frontiers. It required** every **thirty-five male inhabitants, of competent** age, **to** engage and equip **one able-bodied recruit to serve** in **their stead** in said **levies.** Whether at the solicitation **of** his neighbors, **liable** under **this Act, or prompted by** his own devotion to **the service,** or both **combined, we have no** means **of** knowing, but **we find** Van **Arsdale** joining **the levies on** the 2d **of May.** But under an act **of June** 24th **ensuing, which** permitted **privates serving** in the levies to enlist in either of **the continental** battalions belonging to the State Line, **provided they** engaged to serve **for** the war, Van Arsdale with the then common **idea** that this was the more h norable service, took his **discharge from the** levies, and enlisted in the company of **Capt. Henry** Vandebergh (being **the 1st company) of the 5th** New **York regiment, of** which **Marinus Willett was Lieut.-Col.** Commandant, and belonging **to Gen. James Clinton's brigade.** This **brigade** was then in **garrison at** West Point, **and Van** Arsdale's initial service was fatigue duty on the four redoubts at that post, and guard duty at Fort Montgomery ; the latter reviving but too vividly the campaign of 1777, and its great disaster, **many traces of** which were **still visible.** Vandebergh,

who had had command of the company as lieutenant for the four
months since its captain, Rosecrance, became a major, was now
promoted July 1st, and on the 30th, was officially put in command
as captain. Upon the latter date (it having before been given
out that an attack was to be made upon New York City), the New
York brigade was directed to march next morning at sunrise.
They moved accordingly, crossed the Hudson and took up a position below Peekskill. But the object of the advance, which was
merely strategic, having been served, the army again crossed the
river at Verplank's Point, and on August 7th made headquarters
at Clarkstown. Washington had given orders a week previous
for the immediate formation of a corps of Light Infantry, to be
commanded by General Lafayette. It consisted of two brigades,
each of three battalions, and each battalion composed of eight
companies selected from the different lines of the army, by taking
the first or "light company" of each regiment. Capt. Vandebergh's company was included in a battalion under Col. Philip
Van Cortlandt. Gen. Lafayette was at great expense to equip
this corps which was pronounced as fine a body of men as was ever
formed. They were in neat uniform, and each soldier wore a
leather helmet, with a crest of horsehair, and carried a fusil.
The General took command August 7th, and at three o'clock the
next morning the army marched, with the light infantry in the
advance, and proceeded to Orangetown, where and in the vicinity
it lay for some time, in readiness, should Sir Henry Clinton leave
on an expedition eastward or southward, of which there were indications, to strike a vigorous blow at New York. Soon after
occurred the foul treason of Arnold, and the capture, trial and
execution of Major Andre. The light infantry were at Tappan,
October 2d, when this last sad tragedy took place.* Lafayette
felt great pride in this corps, and was at infinite pains to perfect
its discipline, which by the assiduity of the officers he brought to

---

* GEN. LAFAYETTE, upon his last visit to this country, arrived at
Staten Island, on Sunday, August 15, 1824. Capt. Van Arsdale had a
grandson born on the same day. The next morning on landing at the
Battery, the General was received by the Veteran Corps, and passing
along the line, took each member cordially by the hand. Coming to
Capt. Van Arsdale, he looked him intently in the face, as if he knew
him, yet was not quite sure. But the instant the Captain alluded to his
service in the Light Infantry Corps, the General's countenance lightened
up, and there was a full recognition. "Van Arsdale," said he with
emotion, as if the glorious past was flushing his memory, "Van Arsdale,
I remember you well!" Going home, pleased beyond measure, that the
General should recollect him, after a lapse of forty-four years, Capt. Van
Arsdale went to see his little grandson, and being desired to give him
a name, called him *John Lafayette*. This was the late Col. J. Lafayette
Riker, of the 62d New York Volunteers, who in defense of the flag for
which his grandsire sacrificed so much, nobly laid down his life at the
battle of Fair Oaks, May 31, 1862.

high proficiency. **But the** campaign passed without affording him an opportunity to perform any signal **service.** The corps was broken up on November 28th for the **winter,** and the companies returned to their respective regiments.

On December 4th the New York line sailed for Albany to go **into** winter quarters, but, the levies which had joined it, being discharged by order of Gen. Washington, because of a **scarcity** of provisions and clothing, Van Arsdale took leave of his **regiment,** December 15th, much to his disappointment, having enlisted for the war. But he had won the favor of Col. Willett, who was pleased to say that he was "a good soldier and attended to his duties." Except a small gratuity from **the** State, of "Twenty Dollars of the Bills of the new emission," received when he joined the 5th regiment, he returned without any remuneration for his services in this campaign ; but with a patriotism uncooled, and rising superior to mercenary motives, the winter recess was no sooner past when Van Arsdale again joined the levies raised for the defense of the **State, under** Col. **Albert Pawling.** One of the captains was John Burnet, of Little Britain, who had been in the battle **at** Fort Montgomery. **Van** Arsdale entered his company, April 25th, 1781, and was given the position of sergeant, **with ten dollars a** month pay, which was an advance of two dollars. **He was** posted much of the time on the frontier of Ulster County, **where the levies** were billeted on the families, a few in a house, **to protect them** from Indians. These had done but little mischief **in this section of** the State, since the crushing blow inflicted **upon them** by Sullivan's expedition. The principal outrage **had been** committed the last year (1780), when a small **party under** Shank's Ben, on September 17th, attacked the house of Col. Johannes Jansen, in Shawangunk, intending to capture him, but, failing in this, seized and carried off a young woman named Hannah Goetschius, and whom, with one John Mack and his daughter, Elsie, they murdered and scalped in the woods !

But the present year witnessed a **more** formidable invasion. Col. Pawling had sent **out** Silas Bouck and Philip Hine, on a scout, to watch for the enemy. **Near** the Neversink River, they discovered **a large body of Indians and** Tories approaching ; but, then starting back **to give the alarm, were intercepted** by Indian **runners and captured.** The settlements **were** therefore **unprepared for a visit ; when early on** Sunday morning, **August 12th, this savage horde** stole into Wawarsing and began **an attack upon the stone fort.** Being repulsed **with loss, they** departed to plunder and burn a dozen **scattered** dwellings ; many others being saved by the bravery **of the levies** quartered in them. Pursued by Col. Pawling as soon as he could collect a force, they had time **to escape ;** but, **on** September 22d, returned again to burn Wawarsing. On this occasion, also, they first attempted to surprise the fort, but an alarm being given by the sentinel firing his gun, the garrison were warned and the inhabitants fled from their houses and secured themselves. The enemy, again repulsed with a number slain, proceeded to pillage and burn the place. Capt. Burnet was then stationed at a blockhouse at Pinebush (in Mombackus, now town of Rochester), whence he and Capt. Kortright marched towards Wawarsing, but, not being in sufficient force to give battle, turned back. Soon Col. Pawling arrived and they pursued the enemy about 40 miles, being out seven days, but they could not overtake them. There was a private in Van Arsdale's company named George Anderson, who three years before had performed an exploit which marked him as a hero. He and Jacob Osterhout were seized one evening in a tavern at Lackawack, by some Indians and Tories, and carried off towards Niagara. When within a day's march of that place, Anderson, at midnight, effected their release, and with his own hand tomahawked the three sleeping Indians who then had them in charge; then, each taking a gun, provisions, etc., set out with all speed for home, where they arrived exhausted and almost starved, after seventeen days. The State gave Anderson £100 "for his valor." Van Arsdale used to relate this adventure, whence has come the mistaken idea that it happened with himself.*

On Dec. 19th, Van Arsdale's service ended, and he returned home to spend the winter; with a good conscience, doubtless, but still with empty pockets! Yet all looked bright and hopeful, great success had crowned our arms in other quarters; the proud Cornwallis had been humbled, and his splendid army captured. On the opening of 1782, measures were concerted to follow up these successes; the army was maintained, and a body of levies were also raised in this State to afford the usual protection to our frontiers. In these Van Arsdale enlisted on the 27th of April, in the company of Capt. John L. Hardenburgh, of Col. Frederick

*Soon after Anderson's escape. the Indians, in retaliation, as was believed, burnt a house and several barns near Pinebush (in Mombackus), murdered two men, and carried off a third, named Baker, who was never heard of again, and was probably reserved for the worst tortures. Two or three hundred troops then lay at a fort on Honk Hill, under Lt. Col. Newkerk, of McClaughry's regiment, and volunteers being called for, to go out and intercept the Indians who were supposed to be few in number, Lieut. John Graham offered himself, and set out with twenty man. At the Chestnut Woods (now Grahamsville, Sullivan Co.,) they lay in wait for the wiley foe, but were themselves drawn into an ambush, and only two escaped to tell the sad tragedy. Lieut. Graham fell at the first fire. This happened on September 6th, 1778. Three hundred men went out and buried the dead where they fell. They had all been scalped. Graham was an uncle to the lady whom Van Arsdale afterwards married, and a half-brother to Wm. Bodle, Esq., before mentioned.

Weissenfels' regiment. Five days after, he was made sergeant, and served as such **during** that campaign, holding the place of first or orderly sergeant from Sept. 24th. But the season passed in inactivity, and the magazine of provisions at Marbletown being **exhausted**, the levies were disbanded, and on December 28th, Van Arsdale received an honorable and final discharge from the army. **He** laid away **his** musket with a lighter heart than on any former occasion. True **he and** his fellow soldiers *had received no pay during the last three campaigns!* But he had escaped the thousand **perils of the service and was** permitted to see this grevious war practically closed **and** independence secured. Recompense ample, **yet** the State was just to its brave defenders, and soon afterwards paid them for this service, and also those who had been prisoners of war, for their time from the day they were captured **to** the day of their return from captivity.*

There were more times than one, **Van Arsdale** being at home, **when** the farmhouse at Neelytown, upon sudden news of a victory, echoed with cheers long and loud, and witnessed a lively jig, enacted then and there impromptu, with all his early zest for the **dance;** but how buoyant were his spirits now, the bitterness of the struggle being past and the final victory achieved, while **the** future seemed radiant with promise.

The ensuing winter, spent with his brother, was one **of unusual** gayety, and **at a** social party given by his old **friend,** Alexander Bodle, then married and living at La Grange, **he first met with** his future wife, Mary Crawford, a most amiable girl, six years his junior. Escorting **her** home **in** his sleigh, the acquaintance ripened—the bans were published in the church at Goshen, of which her father, **David** Crawford, was an elder; and the Rev. Nathan Ker married them at the hospitable farmhouse, in Walkill, on the 16th of June, **1783.** Van **Arsdale now** left his brother's, where **he had** experienced a kindness almost parental, and with his bride, who ever proved herself a discreet companion, **went to** keeping **house** in **New Windsor. He** had found an occupation suited **to his robust and active temperament.** The owner of the Black **Prince, a vessel** used during the war as a gunboat, but now fitted **up for the** more peaceful service **of** conveying passengers **and freight on** the Hudson, **wanted Van** Arsdale **as** a partner. The latter **assented,** he always **loved the water; it** was moreover

---

* He was entitled to a "Soldier's Right," (500 acres), **in** the unappropriated lands of the State, which was promised each recruit joining the Levies in 1781, to be given **him** as soon after his term of service closed, as the survey could be safely made; but it is traditionary in the family, that thinking it of little value, he neglected to secure it within the time prescribed by law, three years after the war should close. Rights sold for only $50, after **the war.**

an opportunity to begin life respectably with his Polly, **for a living was not so** easily secured just after the war, when the country was impoverished, money scarce and times hard, while he saw **many** of his old comrades in arms wanting employment. **So he** donned the tarpaulin and sailor jacket, and entered **on a calling** in which he was engaged when **the** incident of November **25th, 1783,** occurred; and at **which he became** a veteran, sustaining **the** character of a safe and **skillful captain, and an honest and noble-** hearted man. **Affable to and careful of the passengers who** patronized his packet ; **this in itself was an** advertisement, **and** many making their annual **visit to the City,** either for pleasure or to sell their dairies **or other farm produce, or to** purchase goods (for the day of railroads was **not yet), much** preferred sailing with "Captain John." **His passenger** list was full on the trip preceding **Evacuation Day, but of that** memorable day we need add nothing ; **and the sequel of Capt. Van** Arsdale's life will be briefly told.

After four years the Captain closed his business relations with New Windsor, and removed to New York, taking command of the **"Democrat" for** Col. Henry Rutgers, and where, with the excep- **tion** of brief residences on Long Island and in Westchester County, before his final return to the City in 1811, he made his **home for the rest of** his life. He was granted the freedom of **the City, April** 1st, 1789 ; and shortly after engaged in a different calling, **but five** years later resumed the old one, and successively sailed **(some-** times as part owner), the Deborah—named for his mother—the Packet, Neptune, Rising-Sun, Ambition, Venus **and Hunter. It was** while sailing the Hunter, during the last war **with England, that in coming** out of Mamaroneck Harbor (September 17th, **1813), he narrowly escaped** capture by one of the enemy's vessels; a market **boat which they** had seized and manned, to more easily entrap **ours. The Captain thought** they acted strangely, but dis- covered **their real character only** when they bore down and rounded to, **with intent to** board him. **But the** Captain was **too** quick for **them. Ordering the** passengers **below,** he instantly tacked about, the bullets now flying thick around him, and shout- ing to the foe **to** *fire away, it was not the first time* they had *wasted powder on him,* he was soon beyond their reach, and got in safely, with no other damage than **sails riddled, and a few holes** in the hull. The people ashore, having **heard the firing and** alarmed for the Captain's safety, **were overjoyed, and came out in** small boats to help him in. There **were** several **little incidents** connected with this adventure. **A brave** woman on board, a Mrs. **Wallace,** insisted upon rowing with a sweep, till fairly forced to desist and go below. The cabin-boy when told to go down, de- murred, saying, "Captain, when **your** head **is** off, I'll take the helm." A few days before, the Captain going into the country to buy produce, had told his son David to keel up the vessel and and give it a coat of tallow, which preserved the timbers, kept her tight and helped her sailing. David obeyed orders, but so thoroughly and well, that he ran up a big score for tallow at the store, to the astonishment of his father when he came to see the bill, and who gave David a round reprimand for his extravagance. But after the trial of speed with the enemy, "David," said the Captain, patting his son on the shoulder, "we hadn't a bit too much tallow on to-day!"

Speaking of David, he was in one respect "a chip of the old block," he relished a joke next the best. And so it happened on an occasion, that the schooner lay at Cow Harbor, loading with wood, when a Montauk Indian came aboard, asking a passage to New York. Now the Captain had a kind heart; but had sworn eternal enmity to the whole race of aborigines. His ears filled with recitals of Indian outrages, when scouting on the frontiers; an eye-witness of the cruelties inflicted on peaceable communities by the firebrand and the tomahawk; yes, his soul harrowed at the sight of innocent victims, as they lay in their gore, murdered and scalped; if there was on earth an object at sight of which his very blood boiled, it was an *Indian!* David knew it well, yet the young rogue sent the Indian into the cabin to see the Captain. "What do you want?" asked the latter gruffly. "To go to New York, Captain," said the poor native. "Get out of this, you Indian dog," was his only answer, while the Captain's cudgel at his heels, as he scrambled up the companionway, sent the applicant off at a much livelier gait than "an Indian trot." But then it was that the joke turned on David, when he had to meet the scathing question,—How he *dared* to send an *Indian* into the cabin to him!

But we said the Captain himself enjoyed a joke. In 1821, he and Squire Daniel Riker took a friendly tour, in the latter's gig, as far as Orange County; Mr. V. to see his kindred and acquaintances, and one of his daughters being also there on a visit. Concluding to go as far as Monticello, they set out from Bloomingburgh, the Squire and Deborah in the gig, and the Captain on horseback. Shortly before reaching the Neversink River, the latter stopped to have a shoe set, but told the Squire to drive on and he would soon follow. Now the Squire was a spruce widower of fifty, but Deborah just out of her teens. So on they went reaching the toll-gate in high glee and at a lively pace. The inquisitive gate-keeper had noticed the speed at which they rode, and overheard a tell-tale remark let fall by the Squire, that by driving fast they might reach the Neversink bridge *before the Captain could catch them!* Soon the Captain arrived in seeming haste, and reigning his horse at the gate, inquired of the keeper if he had seen a runaway couple that way ; an old man eloping with his daughter. " Yes, yes," said the man, "they just passed, and were hurrying to reach the bridge before you could catch them ; but you'll do it if you're only smart." " Quick, quick, hand me my change," said the Captain, and spurring his horse, on he went, almost bursting before he could give vent to his laughter ; while the gate-keeper ran in to tell about the wonderful elopement. But on their return, there was a hearty laugh all round, as the gate-keeper took in the situation, and the Captain, with a smirk, remarked, "You see, I caught the runaways." The joke spread, to the merriment of all, but none enjoyed telling it more than the Captain.

In 1816, having quit his old occupation the previous year, and being now sixty years of age, Capt. Van Arsdale was appointed Wood Inspector in the First Ward, a post he held for twenty years ; and which he had previously enjoyed for a short time, in 1812, under a commission from De Witt Clinton, then Mayor. Daily at Peck Slip, he was seen, with his measuring rod in hand, busy at his avocation ; till " Uncle John " became one of the fixed features of the locality. He continued here, indeed, till the use of coal had so far supplanted that of wood, that business dwindled to nothing, and he resigned his office in disgust. He was made a member of the " Independent Veteran Corps of Heavy Artillery," Oct. 6th, 1813. This Corps was organized for the special defense of the City of New York, and for the whole period Mr. Van Arsdale was connected with it (except a short interval), was commanded by Capt. George W. Chapman. Their uniform was a navy blue coat and pantaloons, white vest, black stock, a black feather surmounted red, black hat, and cockade, bootees and side arms yellow mounted. Capt. Van Arsdale took great interest in the corps, rarely if ever missed a parade, and in 1814, for over three months, ending December 4th, was in active service guarding the Arsenal in Elm street, a plot being suspected to blow up the building with its 14,000 stand of arms. On Nov. 25th, 1835, he was promoted to the next position to the commandant, that of First Captain-Lieutenant.

Capt. Van Arsdale had now reached his eighty-first year, he had survived his companion four years, his mental faculties were still good, but his strength was failing ; yet he attended to business till near the last. But borne down by the weight of years, a short illness closed the scene, and the veteran gently passed away, August 14th 1836, at his residence 134 Delancey street. He was interred the next day in the cemetery in First street, with the honors of war, by the corps in which he had held command ; the Napoleon Cadets, Capt. Charles, acting as a guard of honor, and a concourse of citizens paying their last respects. His remains now rest in **Cypress** Hills Cemetery.*

In person Mr. **Van Arsdale** was of **medium** height, stoutly built, erect, and elastic **of foot even** till old age. Always neat in **his person** and dress ; we recall his good-natured chiding, when, an urchin, running in to see Grandpa, heated from our play, and collar, boylike, well sweated down ;—"Go home, you little rascal,' he would say, "You've no collar to your shirt." A democrat of the old school, he was pronounced in his opinions, and no way sparing of opponents. It was in the autumn of 1834, that a friend asked him how the party which that year took the name of *Whig*, got it. "Got it," said the old man, his face kindling with honest indignation, "Smiley, they got it as their fathers, the Cowboys of the Revolution, got their beef,—*they stole it!*" The Captain was then visiting friends in Sullivan County, and was riding out to see his old war-chum Sears. They met on the road, when Mr. V. springing from the wagon, Sears instantly recognized him, and overcome with emotion, threw his arms around him and burst into tears ! How flushed up the faded memories of camp and battle scenes, and dismal **prison** life ; verily a picture for the limner. At this time also, the Captain had the pleasure of visiting Mr. Hugh **Lindsey**, who was captured with him at **Fort** Montgomery ; he died **shortly** after Van Arsdale's **return**. But we have done. The kind father,—filial affection still **cherishes** his memory ; the true friend,—alas, but **few survive to embalm** the friendship so long sundered ; the worthy citizen, whose heart was ever open to the poor and suffering around **him,**—let it suffice that the savor of good deeds is immortal ! But more fitting to close this imperfect tribute to his worth are the apt words of the burial orders, recalling the salient fact in Capt. Van Arsdale's life,—"A tried Soldier of the Revolution !"

---

* CAPT. VAN ARSDALE had five children who reached adult years ; three of whom, his only son before named, and two daughters, yet survive. His eldest daughter, married to the late Alderman James Riker, and long since deceased, was the mother of the writer of this sketch, also of Col. J. Lafayette Riker, named in a preceding note ; another daughter yet survives her husband, the late estimable John Phillips ; another is the widow of Jacob G. Theall, and mother of Mrs. Dr. Jared G. Baldwin, of New York, and a fourth daughter married the la e, much respected, Capt. Andrew Dorgan, of Mobile, whose sons Augustus P. and Lyman Dorgan, are well known merchants at that place. (*See Annals of Newtown*, p. 307.)

MR. DAVID VAN ARSDALE.

This venerable citizen, son of Capt. John Van Arsdale, and to whom some humorous references have been made in these pages, has suddenly ended his pilgrimage, as our last sheet was passing from the press. He died yesterday, (November 14th,) at the age of 87 years. His decease on the very eve of the Centennial, in the observance of which he was expected to take a special part causes the deeper regret; but we forbear remark, while the City Press is teeming with obituaries expressive of respect for his memory.

www.ingramcontent.com/pod-product-compliance
Lightning Source LLC
Chambersburg PA
CBHW031751090426
42739CB00008B/968